D1631454

SEMANTIC THEORY

SEMANTIC THEORY:

A Linguistic Perspective

Don L. F. Nilsen
Arizona State University

Alleen Pace Nilsen
Arizona State University

NEWBURY HOUSE PUBLISHERS, Inc. / Rowley / Massachusetts

C

NEWBURY HOUSE PUBLISHERS, Inc.

 Language Science
Language Teaching
Language Learning

68 Middle Road, Rowley, Massachusetts 01969

ISBN: 0-88377-040-7 (paper)
         0-88377-041-5 (cloth)

Printed in the U.S.A.   First printing: February, 1975

Cover design by Harry Swanson

D
412
NIL

Acknowledgments

We've been very fortunate to have been associated with schools which support linguistic programs and linguistic discussions. We gratefully acknowledge our indebtedness to the University of Northern Iowa and to Arizona State University for providing the kinds of atmosphere under which a book such as this could have been written. More specifically, we appreciate the linguistic brain-storming sessions with Gordon Ford, Val Johnson, Norman Stageberg, and George Tharp at the University of Northern Iowa, and with Barry Alpher, Robert Chubrich, Lee Croft, Frank D'Angelo, Paul Murphy, Jim Ney, and Bill Winn at Arizona State University. We are also grateful to our UNI and ASU classes for their constructive criticism, and to the members of the NCTE Kalamazoo workshop on discourse analysis during the summer of 1973 (where an earlier edition of this manuscript was used as a text) for their very valuable reactions to the material. But most of all we would like to thank J. Donald Bowen of UCLA and Ralph Goodman of UNI for their detailed reading of and reaction to the manuscript. Through their careful attention they were able to catch many errors, inconsistencies, and vaguenesses in the original manuscript. We are extremely grateful for their help and we accept full responsibility for whatever errors and inconsistencies still remain.

TO KELVIN, SEAN, AND NICOLETTE

Foreword

Without question the central fact of language is that it serves as a means of communication between human speakers (and writers), that by means of language people can exchange information. How this is done, how people speak to and understand each other, has been a fascination to scholars for centuries. Yet we know very little of how the process actually works. Contributing to the astonishing fact of human communication is the multiplicity and variety of linguistic systems extant in the world today, some three to four thousand different languages, all of which manage to fulfill the basic communication needs of the groups who use them.

It is generally appreciated that languages are highly abstract and complex sets of symbols and relationships. In some strange way the sequences of sounds men make are correlated with the real world we inhabit, but we are still, after all of our serious study, endeavoring to understand how this happens. Since they all do the same job, what do languages have in common? Since they are not intercomprehensible, how are they different? How can the same information be transmitted by any natural language? What is the nature of meaning and how can it be described and understood? Is language a reliable means of describing the real world, or does it somehow extrapolate one system in terms of another? Is reality perceived directly or is it interpreted in terms of language?

In earlier times many of these questions were asked by poets and philosophers, but now linguists, psychologists, sociologists, anthropologists, physiologists, and scholars of other disciplines are involved in these seemingly esoteric areas of language study. Traditional language scholars were concerned with meaning, but had come up against a blank wall, unable to specify their intuitions with anything approaching scientific rigor. The structuralists concentrated on the physical end of the linguistic spectrum, and the closest they got to semantics was to specify differential (as opposed to referential) meaning, indicating that two terms did or did not have the same meaning. The structuralist methodology handled phonology, but faltered when attempting to handle syntax (by a marriage of intonation and grammar), with semantics still over a distant hill and no serious hope of attaining it in the generation then current. The generativists went a giant step further, recognizing deep structure relations under the surface, which mediated between sounds and meaning, though their assumption of the primacy of syntax in the formulation of a message for transmission has subsequently been questioned. The next logical step was a move toward meaning itself, as a central component of linguistic structure, and modest steps in this direction are being taken.

Meaning is, after all the raison d'être of human communication. Probably hindsight will tell us that the present probes into the area of semantics are preliminary steps, but this is the nature of research. Students in linguistics, in language teaching, and in related disciplines will want to know where we are in semantics, what directions of research are most promising, what we can hope to achieve in the relatively near future.

The Nilsens offer us a carefully thought out organization of human communication from the relevant point of view of semantics. Their efforts are much needed and most welcome. It is timely that an informative and readable "state of the art" paper is directed to the nonspecialist in semantics, complete with evaluative bibliographic reference that will facilitate going further in any of the interesting directions that are sketched out. It will be helpful for the general linguist and ideal for the language teacher who wants to keep abreast of this most relevant advancing frontier in his profession.

But while we look ahead there are workaday problems that the teacher must handle, such as teaching the definitions assigned to vocabulary items, comparing words of similar meanings—within or between languages, understanding the nature of equivalences in the context of linguistic analysis, the avoidance of unclear expression, the appropriate casting of ideas in sentences, the meaning and effect of style, etc. The presentation by the Nilsens of antonomy, synonomy, paraphrase, ambiguity, anomaly, the discussion of semantic features and deep case frames, the potential contributions of a better understanding of linguistic universals: all will help the teacher, will lift his confidence that he can adequately handle the complexities of his field.

There are still important gaps in the theory, questions that need answers and other questions that need to be posed. But this most reluctant level of linguistic structure is beginning to yield, and the tools for semantic analysis are hopefully being assembled. The present study is helpful in telling us where we are and where we will probably go. I welcome its appearance and look forward hopefully to the early prospect of a needed revision.

J. Donald Bowen

Contents

I. Semantics in Linguistics and Other Academic Areas

Many American universities have linguistics departments, but many other colleges and universities have instead a linguistics section or a few individual linguists who are administratively associated with some "non-linguistics" department. Considering the variety of ways that colleges are organized, this is not an especially unusual fact; what is strange is the wide range of departments to which linguistics is attached. It is in departments of English, Foreign Languages, English as a Foreign Language, Speech, Philosophy, Psychology, Phonetics, Education, Anthropology, and Folklore. The logical question to ask is what do these divergent fields have in common. The answer is that all of these areas are concerned with the relationship between the real world and people's use of oral or written symbols designed to represent or to relate to this real world in some way. In other words all these fields are interested in the relationship between deep structure which is the semantics or underlying meaning of words and surface structure which is the oral or phonetic (or the written or graphemic) form of words. This relationship is what linguistics is all about.

One way to look at the relationship between deep and surface structure is in terms of levels. The deepest and most concrete level is the real world itself. The relationship between a human being and this real world is through his experience as related through his senses. What is in a person's mind is not the real world, but rather his perception of the real world which is limited by his senses, and also by his ever-changing value system. As soon as objective facts enter the mind of an individual they are subjectively evaluated and classified. Both the real world and a human being's perception of it can be considered the deep structure in a language model.

In order to communicate concepts and attitudes from one person to another, language is needed. The spoken language and the written language are two aspects of the surface structure. And of the two, the oral language is more basic, more primary, and more closely related to the deep structure than is the written language, which is a somewhat inaccurate or incomplete representation of the spoken language. The over-simplified model which has just been presented can be represented somewhat as follows:

	Written Language
Surface Structure (Language)	
	Spoken Language
	Perception of the World
Deep Structure (Reality)	
	The World

There are many people who would disagree with this particular representation of levels of deep structure. Some linguists would say that deep structure, although it approaches reality, is nevertheless a language phenomenon. But only when deep structure is considered to be an aspect of reality rather than an aspect of language can the base component be considered universal. And this is crucial if we are going to consider all languages and dialects as being basically the same, differing only in manner of expression or surface structure.

This is an issue which will be discussed later; for now let us go on with the application of semantic theory to various academic fields. One of the major issues in the field of philosophy from before the time of Plato until the present day has been the relationship between language and reality. Philosophers have been extremely concerned with what they term "reference" and with the relationship between reference and truth. A popular example in recent philosophical literature is the sentence, "The king of France is bald." Some philosophers argue that this sentence is false, because France has no king, and he can therefore not be bald. Other philosophers argue that the sentence is neither true nor false, but rather, inappropriate because "the king of France" is not a referring expression, and it is impossible to make an assertion about something which does not exist. Still other philosophers argue that "the king of France" *is* a referring expression despite the fact that France has no king. They feel that the sentence would never have been uttered in the first place had the speaker not been referring to someone with the expression "the king of France." The speaker made a mistake, or else he intentionally lied or misled, or else he was using the term "king" in an unusual way. But in any case, he was referring to someone, and there is a strong possibility that the person he is referring to is the *president* (not the king) of France. Those philosophers who consider "the king of France" to be a referring expression would consider the sentence "The king of France is bald" to be a *true* sentence if the person being referred to is indeed bald.

Rather than attempting to settle this issue of whether the sentence under consideration is true or false or just someone's mistake, let us look at some other problems of reference which philosophers have considered and ask these same three questions about the truth of these expressions. Suppose a person makes a statement about Cinderella, a dragon, Tarzan, the Easter Bunny, or Gulliver. Again would we have to say that such statements are meaningless, or true, or false, or inappropriate because they do not refer to anything in the real world? Or should we instead consider the truth and the appropriateness of such statements in terms of some non-real world like fairy tales, legends, folk heroes, traditions, and imaginative literature? If someone asked if we thought Tarzan would cower if he were attacked by a unicorn, we would feel confident to answer, "No, he wouldn't," and we would feel that our statement was truthful, relevant, and appropriate. In fact, we would feel more sure answering this question than a question like, "Would Pearl Buck have cowered if she had been attacked by an antelope?" even though "Pearl Buck" and "antelope" denote real-world objects while "Tarzan" and "unicorn" do not.

Philosophers are very much interested in developing the concept of reference because they see this as a direct link between language and the real world which it represents. If human languages were like animal languages which as far as we know only make references to actual concrete objects, then the matter would be relatively simple. However, human language is capable of creating hypothetical worlds which are only more or less based on the real world. But these hypothetical imaginary worlds are described with much the same terminology as is used in describing the real world. If someone says "Gulliver was a Frenchman," a listener who knows that Gulliver doesn't exist and never did can still respond with, "No he wasn't; that's a false statement." And if an honest and straightforward individual, in justifying his own baldness, states, "The king of France is bald," it would be presumptuous and rude of a listener to say, "That statement is false," or "That statement is inappropriate," because to the speaker it is obviously both true and appropriate.

Appropriateness depends on one of the three basic assumptions of any communication act. That assumption is that a person does not make a statement unless that statement is relevant to the linguistic and nonlinguistic context as he sees it. If this assumption does not hold, then communication necessarily breaks down as it often does in mental institutions or with very young children who have not yet learned to assess the context, including the knowledge of their listeners, in which they are speaking. Just as it is the responsibility of the speaker to utter only sentences which are relevant, it is the responsibility of the listener to determine the relevance of the sentences he hears. It is because both the speaker and listener are striving toward establishing relevance that cryptic and incomplete conversations are interpretable. This means that in at least one sense of the word there is no such thing as a sentence containing a "non-referring" expression. In order to be eligible for placement in a sentence, a noun phrase must be relevant and must therefore be a referring expression, even if it is only referring to a situation invented by the speaker simply for the sake of invention.

But relevance is only one of the three basic components of communication. In order for a discourse to work, not only must it be relevant to the linguistic and non-linguistic context, but also it must contain both old and new information. Here again reference is a significant factor. Practically any sentence spoken or written in any language focuses attention on that aspect of the real or imaginary world which is relevant to the sentence, and then gives new information about the topic which has been brought into focus. Grammarians have long been aware of the fact that a sentence is divided into these two parts. The first part is the old information or what is talked about and the second part is the new information or what is said. They have described the two parts as subject-and-predicate or topic-and-comment or theme-and-rheme. More recent grammarians have described the two parts as old-and-new or as presuppositions-and-assertions. This division into two parts is apparent in the traditional Reed-Kellogg diagrams, the structural immediate constituent diagrams, and the transformational tree diagrams which all begin by making this most-important break between the subject and the predicate.

The reference aspect of language with which philosophers have been dealing is most closely related to the subject part of this dichotomy. The basic purpose of reference is to allow the speaker or writer to zero in on the topic for the benefit of the listener or reader. Communication is basically an informative or educational process. The purpose of an act of communication is to inform the listeners or readers of something they didn't know. In a sense they are students while the speaker is a teacher. One of the most basic educational principles is that the teacher should begin with the known and then go on to the unknown. This explains not only why sentences contain both old and new information, but it also explains why the old information typically comes first and the new information typically comes last in the sentences of most natural languages. (An exception is many of the Malayo Polynesian languages which have predicates first.)

But now let us look at some apparent counter examples to the principle just discussed. Consider the book which has as its first sentence, "The house was dark and dingy and was surrounded by a swamp," or the advertisement which begins with, "Our magnificent product..." or the politician's speech which begins with, "My leftist opponent..." or the scholar's article which begins with, "The replacement of empiricism for introspection in the history of thought...". There is something strange about all these introductions because they do not zero in on old information, i.e., that aspect of the real or imaginary world which is jointly known by the speaker and the listener; nor do they identify the subject which the speaker intends to talk about in the predicate or the last part of the sentence.

Each of these subjects is deviant in that it assumes joint knowledge which in fact is not present. This is not to say that such sentences are inappropriate or ineffective or that they were not devised consciously and carefully; nor are such sentences rare.

In fact, the really effective author, debater, politician, or scholar very carefully balances the old and new information in his sentences, not primarily on the basis of what he knows to be old and new information for his audience, but rather on the basis of the communicative effect he wishes to achieve. The writer who begins a novel with, "The house was dark and dingy," is attempting to create the impression that he is already on intimate terms with the reader. He is giving the impression that the author and reader share more information than they actually do. Furthermore, by using this device he is able to begin the novel in the midst of the action rather than at the beginning.

The advertiser puts the adjective "magnificent" in the subject rather than in the predicate part of his sentence in order to fool his listener into thinking that this is already shared information, and therefore does not need to be supported by evidence. The motives of the politician are similar to the motives of the advertiser, except that this particular politician chooses a term which will create a negative impression since he is referring to his opponent, while the advertiser chooses a term which will create a positive impression since he is referring to his own product.

The last example, "The replacement of empiricism for introspection in the history of thought..." does even more than the previous sentences to create the intended impression. This type of a beginning assumes a tremendous amount of shared information on the part of the writer and his audience. It implies that empiricism has replaced introspection, and that this replacement has occurred not in one scholarly field but in many, and it implies that the audience knows what the terms "empiricism," and "introspection," and "history of thought" mean. When an author packs information which the listener does not comprehend into the subject part of the sentence, one effect will be a widening of the intellectual distance between the author and the audience. The listener feels that the author expects him to know whatever information is placed in the subject part of the sentence, and if he is unfamiliar with this information, he considers himself stupid in relation to the speaker.

Therefore packing too much information into the subject component of a sentence can have the effect of establishing a superior or presumptuous relationship between the author and his audience, while packing too much information into the predicate component of a sentence can have the opposite effect of establishing a humble or possibly a condescending relationship. The success of a writer relates to the skill with which he judges the proportion of old and new information for each communication act.

In the communication process, the amount and type of relevance can also be controlled to create special effects. In advertising, a product like life insurance (which when really thought about leaves the purchaser with a squeamish feeling) can not be successfully promoted on its own terms. So it is advertised in terms of automobile safety or a feeling of security or family love. In similar fashion, cigarettes are advertised by a statement about the freshness of springtime or the invigorating air of the desert. A particular toothpaste is said to surround a person with a "ring of confidence" that will allow him to ski successfully down suicide run. A politician may bring ethnic, sex, religious, personal, and health factors into a campaign either as negative factors against his opponent or as positive factors for himself, although these factors may have no bearing whatever on the performance of duty in office. A scholar may casually name-drop in an effort to create the impression of a greater relationship between a respected authority and his thesis than actually exists. Everyone engaged in communication is continually manipulating this balance between old information, new information, and relevance.

In addition, there is a related type of selection process involving paraphrase. It is constantly in use during a communication act. A difference in the distribution of old and new information and/or the varying of the amount or kind of relevance of a particular fact to a particular conversation does not change the truth value of the discourse. For example, the statement, "The quick brown fox was about to leap on the rabbit," has the same truth value as does the sentence, "The brown fox which was about to leap on the rabbit was quick," or "The quick fox which was about to leap on the rabbit was brown." Although all three sentences have the same truth value, the distribution of old and new information, and in fact the relevance, of these three sentences are not the same. In this book all sentences which have the same truth value will be called paraphrases, even though there are no two sentences of any language, or of any pair of languages, which communicate exactly the same thing.

It is an oversimplification to say that the communication process is merely involved in using language to communicate information about the real world because for any real or imaginary world action, state, or event there would be an infinite number of sentences that could be used to report that action, state, or event. This is saying that there are truthfully an infinite number of paraphrases. Yet in an actual communication situation, there may be only a few (possibly only one) sentences that will create the desired effect. The communication process is therefore an extremely selective process with the speaker or writer choosing that one sentence out of the infinite paraphrase possibilities which will be most effective in achieving his purpose.

The difference between good and bad speakers and writers is not necessarily that they are relating to a different real world or that they are perceiving this real world differently, but rather that the good communicator is better at selecting the most appropriate sentences from their fellow paraphrases. This selection affects not only the distribution of old and new information, and the amount and kind of relevance as described above, but it also affects the style, tone, and emphasis of the sentence, and therefore its role within the discourse. Matters of style and tone are very largely determined by the selection of individual lexical items. The good writer and the good speaker always seem to know the precise expression that is most appropriate for a particular context. Success is largely determined by a knowledge of the qualities of each word. These word qualities will be discussed later as semantic features.

The emphasis of a sentence is determined largely by its form and structure, i.e., what transformations have been applied to it or what transformations could be applied to it. The selection of one sentence over its transformational counterparts can affect not only emphasis, but also the distribution of old and new information, and occasionally it can also affect the style and/or tone of the discourse. Transformations can even affect the nature of the speech act itself, for example changing a statement from an information-giving event into a question which is an information-requesting event or a command which is an action-evoking event.

This brings us to the philosophical question of the nature of communication. Various philosophers have discussed the question of whether there is such a thing as private language, or whether all human language is intended, or at least designed, to pass information from one person to another. One view is that language is a particular kind of performance intended not to communicate so much as to get things done. The issue is whether language should be considered as a process of thought, a process of communication, or a process of social interaction.

Clearly language is used in all three ways, but in this book it will be considered basically a process of communication rather than a process of thought or a process of social interaction. Supporting this view that language is basically designed to communicate between individuals is the fact that when someone thinks or talks to himself, his language still contains the complete pronoun system which separates the first person speaker from the second person listener and the third person subject. And although marriage ceremonies and the granting of permission and many other actions are basically linguistic actions, it is still the primary purpose of language to communicate the fact that the action has taken place. The linguistic phenomenon is not the action; instead it is an acknowledgment of the action.

The primary purpose of language is to establish for the communicators a particular relationship with the real world in terms of reference. When the audience knows some but not all of the qualities of the referent, then an incomplete relationship exists and it is the purpose of communication to provide additional qualities of the referent for the audience. This is true not only of a sentence like "John is tall," in which the audience can add the quality, "taller than average or expected," to the inventory of qualities already known about the referent "John." But it is also true of a sentence like "John walked somberly," in which the quality of somberness is attributed to an action—John's walking. And it is furthermore true of a sentence like "I now pronounce you man and wife," in which the referent "you" acquires a new quality, i.e., being married, as a result of the ceremony being performed.

In the above examples the purpose of the communication was to tie together the real world and the language used to talk about it. But in literature a slightly different situation exists in that the distance between the real world and the language is often broadened. Part of the broadening is a result of the fact that much good literature is in the realm of fiction or historical fiction which is semi-fiction. The definition of fiction is that it is untrue; it is one step removed from the real world.

When symbolism and metaphor are used in folk literature, the effect is usually a closing of the gap between the language and the real world because the symbolism highlights well-known semantic features that two items have in common. Often the common features are so well known that the reader or listener is unaware of the fact that he has gotten an idea through a metaphor. We call these "dead metaphors," and the language is full of them, for example, the *eye* of a needle, a *head* of lettuce, and a *thumbnail* sketch. But when fresh metaphors are used in original literature, there is usually a widening of the distance between the language and the real world it represents. This distance results from the fact that when a listener or a reader meets a new metaphor. he must first interpret the literal meaning and then search in his mind for the way this literal meaning can be reinterpreted and applied to the situation being described. Original metaphors attract attention to themselves because they make the reader work harder at decoding. And when the reader is successful in bringing the original metaphorical language to bear on the real-world situation then the communication is very satisfying because the receiver has been forced to travel the same mental path as the producer. A similar result occurs when such authors as e.e. cummings or Lewis Carroll broaden the gap between the real world and communications about it by intentionally using syntactic or semantic anomalies. Their deviation from the normal is linquistically interesting because only by knowing the regular patterns of sentences and the regular meanings of words is it possible for the writer in the first place and the reader in the second place to get at the appropriate meanings. And still another way in which literature broadens the gap between language and the real world is by using a kind of language which is highly subjective and open to individual interpretation. All of these different situations can be understood through the concept of semantic features which will be discussed later in relationship to subjective and objective meanings and the type of feature shifting which goes on as a part of personification, deification, or any other type of metaphor. The special features of chronology, formality, or geographical region that are part of a word will also be discussed as part of semantic features.

One effect of the widening of the gap between the real world and its linguistic representation is that the truth of the resultant literature is difficult to determine. Good literature normally describes what could happen given a particular context. It doesn't really matter that the details of the context and of the events are untrue. The point is that they *could* be true because they are highly relevant to the context. Literature, therefore, tends to obscure the differences between fiction, historical fiction, and non-fiction. It can do this because its purpose is to create a consistent and meaningful impression. Literature must *seem* real; it is beside the point whether it is in fact real or imagined. This is where the field of literature differs from the field of history or science or most other fields. In these latter cases, the gap between the real world and the language is much smaller, since the writing is expository rather than creative. For example, in a history book or a science book the language must *be* true no matter what the effect is or how unlikely the outcome appears.

Psychology is an academic field which, like literature, deals with the subjective aspect of language. Psychologists are interested in perception, and since perception is an individual phenomenon, psychologists have developed techniques to find out how people differ in their perception of words. In general psychologists are attempting to arrive at better systems for determining the semantic features of words, and they are developing better definitions of such concepts as synonymy, antonymy, phonetic similarity, etc. for psychological use in both normal and pathological investigations.

Psychologists are also interested in how language is learned, and they are attempting to determine how much and what kind of language structure is innate. Obviously there is something about the speech process that is inherent since all children tend to learn a remarkably complex language system at basically the same rate regardless of individual differences such as IQ, and despite the fact that in many cases the language they hear is largely the inaccurate language of their peers. Psychologists agree that the human brain is different from the non-human brain both in quantity and quality, but they differ on the amount and type of information that they feel is present in the human brain at birth. Some psychologists hold the view that language learning is the result of a stimulus-response mechanism. Most psychologists holding this view feel that language itself can be a stimulus to produce more sophisticated kinds of responses than are typically produced by real-world stimuli. This language, or thought, or whatever, which functions both as the response to real-world stimuli, and as the stimulus to more sophisticated thought process, is termed mediational response. Its nature is largely unkown, but it would seem that further work on semantic features and syntactic relationships will shed additional light on the subject.

In studying human language development, psychologists have also attempted to investigate the ways in which human communication and nonhuman, or animal, communication differ. Here then is a three-way interrelationship between linguistics, psychology, and zoology. Animal communication is often amazingly complex and sophisticated in communicating on such topics as sex, fear, danger, territorial dominance, food, and motherhood. Almost all domestic animals can be taught to respond to human language commands. And many different birds such as parrots, parakeets, and minah birds have been taught to mimic human languages. A few animals have even been taught to appropriately produce a small number of human language sounds in relation to the real world objects represented by those particular human sounds. But even more amazing is the fact that chimpanzees which were taught several dozen words in sign language and also in plastic tokens, were able to put these "words" into meaningful sets similar to the very early sentences of human children.

The really significant factor in animal language is the semantics or the meaning and not the phonology. For example, the dance of the honeybee with its high meaning content which tells the other bees about the kind of honey found, the distance and the direction it is from the hive, and the obstacles which will be encountered has a low phonological content, but yet it is much more significant than is the mimicry of a parakeet with its high phonological content and low meaning content. Animals can communicate a truth and they can also lie, as when a bird feigns a broken wing to keep an enemy from its nest, or when an opossum plays dead, or when a dog's bark is bigger than its bite. The whole concept of protective coloring is intended to mislead a person into thinking an animal is something it is not, such as a leaf, a stem, or a flower. In the case of the racoon, the coloring confuses an attacker about the actual placement of the racoon's eyes.

These examples show that animal communication, both conscious and unconscious, is extremely varied and extremely sophisticated. But human language has a dimension that is never present in animal communication. Whereas human language can widely be separated from the real world it represents in space, or in time, or on subjective evaluation, or even in imaginative or hypothetical constructs, this is not possible for animal communication.

One of the main purposes of this book is to investigate the meaning component of language in terms of the relationship between language and the real world which it in some way represents. Since our training is in linguistics, we have assumed that this relationship between form and meaning is a linguistic phenomenon. However it belongs equally to everyone who uses language as a tool of communication. Its formal study is important to the philosopher, the psychologist, the zoologist, the writer, the literary critic, the anthropologist, the educator, and the sociologist. Its practical application is important to the business man writing advertising copy, the politician writing speeches, the instructor teaching English or foreign languages, the geographer plotting regional dialects, the historian charting chronological dialects, the dramatist recreating individual dialects, the mathematician setting up formal and rigorous systems, and the speech pathologist working with communication problems.

The fact that semantic theory is part of all these disciplines does not mean that it is a general rather than a specialized field. It simply means that many more people are contributing to its development. The rest of this book is devoted to showing some of the most promising findings which have resulted from these multiple efforts.

II. Semantics in American Linguistics: A Historical Perspective

Every human language is designed to tell about the real world, yet the real world has an infinite number of things and relationships between things while each human language has a more or less set number of terms to refer to these things and their relationships. Furthermore, a human language is often separated from the things it communicates about by space and time. This necessitates using a secondary highly arbitrary system of articulatory or graphic symbols to represent those aspects of the real world which are relevant to the conversation but not in the direct environment of the people communicating.

These factors make for a somewhat loose relationship between any human language and the real world which it attempts to represent. The looseness of this relationship is shown by the fact that the same real-world statement can be made in such a wide variety of ways. Even onomatopoetic words are not the same from language to language. Not all dogs say "bow-wow" nor all cats "meow." And an international display at the Battle Creek, Michigan headquarters of Kellogg's cereal company showed that even Rice Krispies change their sound from language to language. Only in English do they say, "Snap, Crackle, and Pop!"

Throughout history, grammarians have been concerned both with the spoken and written forms of language and with the meanings which these spoken and written forms represent. However, the relationship between meaning and language has been difficult to investigate. As a result this relationship has often been misunderstood and misrepresented. For example, traditional grammarians used meaning as a way of defining some parts of speech. They said, "A noun is the name of a person, place, or thing," "A verb shows action or state of being," and "A sentence expresses a complete thought."

But in the 1930's, thinking began to change with a new generation of scholars known as structural linguists. The structuralists were uniquely American. Many of them came to linguistics through the field of anthropology where they were studying the cultures of American Indians. In order to do this they had to learn the Indian languages which were not written down and which had grammatical patterns that were entirely different from English and from other Indo-European languages.

The difference in the working methods and the goals between American and European linguists caused the Americans to break with traditional thinking. They rejected the idea that Latin was the standard by which all languages should be judged. And they rejected the traditionalist's way of defining parts of speech by meaning. They made a distinction between the categories that words belong to and the function or the role that words play in sentences. And because many of the structuralists were studying languages that had never been written down, they rejected the idea that written language is the primary or most important part. Instead they said that speech was basic and written language was at best only an incomplete and often inaccurate attempt at preserving speech. By putting emphasis on spoken rather than written language, the structuralists increased the importance in linguistic study of phonology, which is the sound system of a language.

Much of the structuralist's literature was concerned with the controversy of whether or not meaning should or could play a role in a linguistic description. The general conclusion was that although meaning was important, there was no adequate way to handle it in a truly scientific or rigorous manner. They therefore tried to find a way of excluding meaning from their analyses. However they did use meaning in a rather trivial way to help in developing their phonological descriptions. For example when two words or the same word pronounced by two different speakers sounded slightly different as do *caught* and *cot* in some dialects, phoneticians decided that because of the difference in meaning the contrast was important and should therefore be labelled as phonemic. But if the words meant the same thing and no examples of these contrasting vowel sounds being used to show different meanings could be found, then the contrast would be considered just a matter of human variation and labelled as phonetic or insignificant.

The structuralists planned that as their work continued they would progress to different types of analyses. They considered language to be analyzable at three levels: phonology, morphology, and syntax. They did not include semantics as one of their goals. They began with phonology because they felt that only with a thorough understanding of this would it be possible for them to move on to morphology which is the study of words and their internal structure. And then they could move on to syntax, which is the study of how words are put together. One of the important books based on this philosophy of phonology first, then morphology, and then syntax was Archibald Hill's 1958 *Introduction to Linguistic Structures: From Sound to Sentence in English.* Another important phonologically based grammar was *An Outline of English Structure* (1951) by George L. Trager and Henry Lee Smith, Jr. Among the structuralists who made morphology and syntax a more basic part of their analysis was Charles C. Fries who outlined his grammar in *The Structure of English*, 1952. Three other important books in this model were *A Course in Modern Linguistics* (1958) by Charles F. Hockett, *An Introduction to Descriptive Linguistics* (1955) by H.A. Gleason, and *The Structure of American English* (1958) by W. Nelson Francis.

In the study of morphology, meaning was again used as a means to an end rather than as an area to be studied for its own sake. In a system analogous to the one distinguishing phonemic and phonetic sounds, structural linguists worked out a way to identify the important parts of words. Words were divided into morphemes which are either words or parts of words which convey meaning and can not be further subdivided without losing meaning. For example, *cars* is made up of two morphemes. The first is the word *car* and the second is the -*s* which carries the idea of plural. But the word *automobiles* has three morphemes. The first is the word *auto* meaning self, the second is the word *mobile* meaning moving, and the third is the -*s* meaning plural.

The structuralists working with morphology developed Immediate Constituent analysis in which a sentence was broken into two smaller constituents which were in turn broken into two still smaller constituents and so on until the ultimate constituents, that is the morphemes, were reached. They used various methods of illustrating their analyses including labelled bracketing, angular lines, and Chinese boxes where smaller and smaller boxes appeared inside a large box.

One of the important linguists working in structural grammar was Zellig Harris at the University of Pennsylvania. He began experimenting with transformations to see if he could discover what grammatical relationships held between items co-occurring in the same sentence. One of his students, Noam Chomsky, further developed the idea of transformations into a new model of grammar. Chomsky's first important book *Syntactic Structures* which appeared in 1957 was an attempt to explain grammatical relationships among related sentences. He was not specifically looking at meaning. It just happened that many of the related sentences which he used were paraphrases of each other.

This new grammar was called Transformational because one of its main aspects was the treatment of the relationship between a kernel sentence and its transformed counterparts. Transformationalists believed that the syntax, the way in which words were arranged, was the base and that there were morphophonemic transformations to allow the linguist to reach the surface structure or the phonology of a sentence. And there were other transformations, most of which did not change meaning, to allow the linguist to reach the deep structure or the semantics of a sentence.

The effect of the transformational model was twofold. First it considered the base of language to be one step deeper in abstraction than did the previous model in that it concentrated on syntax rather than morphology. And second it laid the foundation for a scientific study of semantics. By developing a series of grammatical transformations, the transformational linguists could for the first time explain why the co-occurrence restrictions and often the meanings of a regular statement and its corresponding negative, imperative, question, passive, gerundive, infinitive, relative, and other forms were the same. The transformational model provided the machinery necessary for handling a certain kind of paraphrase relationship, the syntactic paraphrase, in which two sentences have basically the same elements but not necessarily in the same order. And since this model was deeply concerned with co-occurrence relations, it also became concerned with the semantic features inherent in certain words and the concordance of these features with the features of other words. It is when these features are incompatible that co-occurrence violations come about.

Most linguists today are convinced that an adequate theory of grammar must deal not only with phonology, morphology, and syntax, but with semantics as well. However there is uncertainty as to how much paraphrase can be handled in an adequate model. There is also some disagreement as to whether the most efficient and effective level to serve as the base should be syntax or semantics; and in case the level of semantics is chosen to be the base, there is disagreement as to whether this semantic base can best be stated in terms of deep cases or in terms of semantic features. Both of these types of analysis will be discussed later. For now it is sufficient to say that in the history of American linguistics, new models of grammar have always been developed on the framework provided by the old. There has been a logical progression from the study of spoken Indian languages to a concentration on phonology, then on to morphology and then to syntax. The insights gained have finally allowed linguists to begin working on the semantic level of language which in one sense is the most abstract level because it is the hardest to see and measure, since it is a phenomenon that takes place within the human mind. But in spite of this difficulty, the role of semantics in linguistic study has changed within the last forty years from that of an unwanted intruder to that of the central character in a number of significant models. The transformational model started linguists thinking about the meaning or deep structure of sentences, and the models that have been proposed since the transformational model have taken linguists into deeper and deeper and more and more abstract analyses. Perhaps there is no theoretical limit on the depth of this kind of analysis, but certainly there's a practical limit. However much work still remains to be done before even this practical limitation is reached.

The present book attempts to indicate what types of problems should be explored in a semantic theory and which theoretical models have been most successful in considering these problems. In very broad terms, an adequate grammar must be able to indicate which strings are grammatical, that is are syntactically and semantically well formed, and which are ungrammatical. Furthermore, it should be able to give some indication of whether a sentence is likely to be used by a native speaker, that is, is it acceptable or would it have very small chance of appearing in a natural conversation, that is, is it unacceptable even though it is grammatical? An adequate grammar should also be able to tell whether or not the meaning of a sentence, or in fact a discourse, is analyzable. And it should be able to tell whether two parts of a sentence or discourse are redundant or contradictory. It should also be able to indicate if a particular sentence makes no sense, that is, is it semantically anomalous having zero readings. If it has one reading, an adequate grammar would label it as unique, and if it has more than one reading it would label it as ambiguous. This adequate grammar should also be able to explain: the relationship between various sentences which have the same co-occurrence restrictions, such as between an affirmative sentence and its corresponding negative; whether or not two words are synonyms or antonyms and whether or not they belong to the same part of speech; how the words in a sentence relate to each other; when two sentences are paraphrases of each other. If the grammar is really significant, it will be able to use universal symbols so that it can explain paraphrase not only between two sentences of the same language, but between two sentences of different languages.

The rest of this book is devoted to such questions as these. No guarantee is made that the person who reads it will be able to resolve all semantic problems—or any semantic problems for that matter. The most that can be expected is that the reader will be made aware of some of the problems and of some of the solutions that have been suggested. Semantics as a young and emerging discipline is dynamic and exciting. Nevertheless, as grammarians gain deeper and deeper insights into the nature of semantics they usually find that earlier semantic models are in some way incomplete or inadequate. Therefore do not read this book in an attempt simply to find solutions to problems; read it in an attempt to find more and deeper problems.

III. Various Semantic Models

Before going on with recent developments in semantics, we'll review the terms which have been and are now in use in the field, not so much because they are important in themselves, but because the concepts behind the terms are important, and the existence of the terms shows the kind and the amount of work that has been done.

When a person is trying to communicate, the intended meaning exists in that person's mind. It comes to the surface either through speech or through writing. In either case there are complications which might interfere with the intended communication. These can occur with either a single word or with an entire sentence. The problems in speech are not necessarily the same problems as will occur in writing. For example in writing there might be confusion caused by homographs which are words written with the same characters but having different meanings and different origins. Since homographs are pronounced the same, it is appropriate to also call them homophones. The nouns *bank* as in "I'm putting my money in the bank," and "She was sitting on the river bank," are both homographs and homophones because they are written and pronounced the same. However, the three words *their, there,* and *they're* are not homographs because their spelling is different. But they are homophones (at least in some dialects) because they sound the same. A cover term, which is the word most commonly used for this concept, is homonym. Homonyms are words which have different meanings but which sound the same regardless of their spelling. Words which are spelled the same but which have different pronunciations and different meanings are called heteronyms, for example, the verb *lead* as in "I will lead you there," and the noun *lead* as in "I broke the lead in my pencil."

If there are sentences instead of words which have the same pronunciation and/or spelling, but different meanings they are labelled ambiguous. Just as words can be homophonous, sentences can be phonologically ambiguous. For example, "He said he was a bee feeder," sounds very much like "He said he was a beef eater." And just as words can be homographous, sentences can be orthographically ambiguous. The purpose of most punctuation is to try to bring to writing the intonation and pause patterns of speech. Without these helps, many sentences would be orthographically ambiguous. Even so, there are still sentences where punctuation can not make clear which of several readings is intended. For example, "The photographs were taken by the main office," could mean that someone in the main office was the photographer or that the photographs were taken in the vicinity of the main office, or that the photographs had been dropped off at the main office. With this sentence, as with many others, in actual use the intended meaning would probably come through because of the speaker's intonation or body language, or because of the real-world situation which the speaker and the listener are both aware of. But in writing, none of these things are present in the same degree so that written sentences tend to be ambiguous more often than spoken sentences. A sentence commonly given as an example of this kind of ambiguity is the headline or telegraph message, "Ship sails tomorrow." There is no way that punctuation can tell a reader whether *ship* is the verb and *sails* is the noun or *sails* is the verb and *ship* is the noun.

Words which have similar meanings but different spellings and sounds are called synonyms, for example *trousers* and *pants*. Sentences having similar meanings but different words are called paraphrases, for example, "John came by plane," and "My best friend arrived on a 707 jet."

But what about a pair of words like *borrow* and *lend*? The sentences, "John lent me $5.00," and "I borrowed $5.00 from John," refer to the same real-world situation. Therefore in a sense the words *borrow* and *lend* must have the same meaning and might therefore be considered synonyms. More specifically, such pairs as *borrow-lend, buy-sell, give-take,* etc. are called converses, meaning that they occur with the same words (e.g., John, me, and $5.00), and have basically the same meanings, but they impose a surface structure constraint that the words must be in a different linear order. They cause different words to end up as subjects, objects, and prepositional phrases. This means that different words are emphasized, but the meanings are the same. So in a way it is possible to consider such terms as *lend* and *borrow* both as synonyms and as antonyms without being contradictory.

Words which are alike or very similar in all three areas of meaning, pronunciation, and spelling but which occur in different languages are called cognates, for example Italian *studiare* and English *study.* At the opposite extreme from these very similar words are words which are different in meaning, pronunciation, and spelling. These words are called antonyms as exemplified by the pair *freeze-melt.* But it is not enough to say simply that the meanings of two antonyms are different, since there are some semantic constraints on the amount and type of difference. First, antonyms must be of the same syntactic and semantic class. And second, within this class they must be polar opposites. More will be said about antonyms in a later chapter.

The graph on the following page summarizes this discussion of the interrelationships between the terms relating semantics, phonology, and orthography.

There are several approaches to the study of semantics. Some of these are full-fledged rigorous models presenting machinery for the treatment of semantic matters, while others are merely statements about semantics and ways of dealing with it. In the United States early semantic models included general semantics, Whorfian semantics, and semantic differentiation. More recent developments are logical and mathematical semantics, interpretive semantics, generative semantics, case grammar, and Chafe grammar.

Term for Words:	Example:	Meaning:	Phonology:	Orthography:	Term for Sentences:
Cognate	English: study Italian: studiare	Similar	Similar	Similar	————
Homograph	bank-bank	Different	Same	Same	Ambiguity
Homophone	their-there	Different	Same	Different	Ambiguity
Heteronyn	lead-lead	Different	Different	Same	————
Synonym	pants-trousers	Similar	Different	Different	Paraphrase
Converse	lend-borrow	Similar	Different	Different	Paraphrase
Antonym	freeze-melt	Same class but polar opposites	Different	Different	————

(Homograph and Homophone are grouped under **Homonym**.)

GENERAL SEMANTICS:

When the lay person hears the term "semantics," he probably thinks of general semantics which is concerned with very practical matters such as the improvement of communication through better word usage. General semanticists work basically with performance rather than competence. The kind of work done in this model can be seen from the titles of some of the important books written by general semanticists. They are listed chronologically. *The Meaning of Meaning* by C.K. Ogden and I.A. Richards (1923); *Language in Thought and Action* by S.I. Hayakawa (1939, third edition, 1972); *Philosophy in a New Key* by Susanne K. Langer (1948); *Words and What They Do to You* by Catherine Minteer (1952); *Science and Sanity* by Alfred Korzybski (1958); and *Semantics and Common Sense* by Louis B. Salomon (1966).

It can be seen from the types of issues which the general semanticists deal with that they have had an influence on later models. However it should be pointed out that general semantics is an informal model and is considered by modern linguists to be outside the scientific investigation of language.

WHORFIAN SEMANTICS:

In the early 1900's an anthropologist by the name of Benjamin Lee Whorf developed the idea that the way humans perceive the world around them is influenced by the language they happen to speak. Taken literally, this means that if we speak a language that is different from someone else's then we will see the world differently than that person does. People use Whorf's idea as an explanation of one of the causes of international misunderstanding and strife. And just recently feminists have been referring to the Whorfian hypothesis as supporting their desire to change parts of the English language which they feel make the male seem more important than the female.

Chapter Ten of Edward Sapir's *Language* which was published in 1921 gives a good statement of Whorf's ideas. And in 1956, John B. Carroll edited *Language Thought and Reality: Selected Writings of Benjamin Lee Whorf.*

SEMANTIC DIFFERENTIATION:

A significant semantic model which has developed within the field of psychology is termed semantic differentiation. Informants are asked to rate words along a number of subjective scales designed to help the researcher determine the connotations of a particular word. For example, on a seven-place scale, a person would have to indicate whether "father" would be considered happy or sad, hard or soft, fast or slow, etc. Seventy-six such scales were originally proposed, but this number is by no means set. These seventy-six scales can be grouped into categories according to whether the scale is a test of some sort of evaluation (good-bad, optimistic-pessimistic, kind-cruel, etc.), potency (hard-soft, strong-weak, severe-lenient, etc.), stability (stable-changeable, cautious-rash, orthodox-heretical, etc.), tautness (angular-rounded, straight-curved, sharp-blunt, etc.), novelty (new-old, usual-unusual, youthful-mature, etc.), receptivity (interesting-boring, sensitive-insensitive, savory-tasteless, etc.) aggressiveness (agressive-defensive, etc.) and miscellaneous (ornate-plain, near-far, tangible-intangible, etc.). The informant is forced to make a ranking for each item. Thus, he is forced to rate a word like "father" somewhere on the seven-point scale ranging, for example, from angular to rounded, and there is always the problem that different informants are using different intuitive criteria in making such judgments. Even those scales which are extremely relevant to the terms being analyzed are subjective. The subjectivity which is being measured is very elusive. This is the chief value as well as the chief limitation of this particular method. A good statement on this model is *The Measurement of Meaning* by Charles E. Osgood, George J. Suci, and Percy H. Tannenbaum (1957).

LOGICAL AND MATHEMATICAL SEMANTICS:

For quite some time specialists in symbolic logic and set theory have been working with various issues which are highly significant to the work of semantically oriented linguists. Recent work in semantic theory has borrowed heavily from these two fields.

Logicians have been very much interested in denotation; in contrasting, for instance, a vague concept like "gryphon" which has no concrete referent in the real world with a concept like "horse" which has a definite referent. They make the distinction between intensional meaning, which is the semantic qualities of a word, and extensional meaning, which is the way a word extends or relates to the real world. They are also interested in whether an expression represents an accidental or purposeful action. And one of their most important interests concerns the analaticity of a statement. If the truth of a statement can be determined wholly by a knowledge of the meanings of its parts, then it is said to be analytic. A sentence which does not have this quality is said to be synthetic. A synthetic sentence cannot be shown to be either logically true (tautological), or logically false (contradictory) by its internal structure. A contradiction is a statement in which two or more parts of the internal structure are incompatible with each other. For example, the sentence, "Kings, presidents, magistrates, and dictators are rulers," is tautological because if you know the meanings of the words *kings, presidents, magistrates, dictators,* and *rulers,* you can correctly judge the sentence to be true. By the same process if you know the meanings of the words *peasants* and *rulers*, you can correctly judge the sentence, "Peasants are rulers," to be contradictory. Both of these decisions were arrived at through studying the internal structure of the sentences. But with the synthetic sentence, "Elmer is a ruler," there is nothing in the sentence itself which will enable us to judge its truthfulness or falseness. Instead we have to know something about the real world and about Elmer.

Logicians have also been very interested in sentence analysis. Consider, for example, the sentence "John hit Mary." In this sentence "hit" is described as a two-place predicate because it requires two nouns: a subject and an object. In terms of logical predicates, this sentence could be analyzed as follows: hit_{xy}. human_x. male_x. name_{xz}. John_z. human_y. female_y. name_{yw}. Mary_w. And this would be read as follows: "x hit y, and x is human, and x is male, and x has the name z, and z is John, and y is human, and y is female, and y has the name w, and w is Mary." This type of analysis is similar to recent proposals by some linguists in which such logical predicates as "human," and "male," are thought of as semantic features. It is also similar to some recent analyses in that it considers the predicate as the central word in the sentence.

Logicians are also working on identifying words as members of particular sets or categories, and they are trying to measure the effects of quanitifers such as *all, no,* and *there exists;* conjunctions such as *and* and *or,* casual relationship words such as *if...then,* and *if and only if,* and mathematical terms such as *equals, is greater than,* and *is greater than or equal to.* Such concepts as reflexivity, transitivity, and reciprocity are also being worked on. For example, two words are said to be reflexive if one refers back to the other, as in *"I cut myself."* A transitive expression in the mathematical sense is one which extends a quality, for example such expressions as *tall, old, fat,* etc. in that if A is taller than B, and B is taller than C, then A is automatically taller than C. In contrast, the expression *friend* is not transitive. A could be a friend of B, and B a friend of C without A being a friend of C. Two expressions are reciprocal if their positions can be reversed in reference to the predicate. For example, if A is a neighbor of B, B is a neighbor of A. In the sentence, "John married Mary," *marry* is a reciprocal predicate, but in the sentence, "The priest married them," *marry* is not reciprocal.

People working in logical and mathematical semantics have devised an elaborate shorthand for dealing with the various concepts they are interested in. Some good books in which these concepts have been developed are *Machine Translation of Languages* edited by William N. Locke and A. Donald Booth (1955), *Handbook of Mathematical Psychology* edited by R. Duncan Luce, Robert R. Bush, and Eugene Galanter (1963), and *Mathematical Linguistics in Eastern Europe* by Ferenc Kiefer (1968).

Books on logical semantics include *Word and Object* by Willard Van Orman Quine (1960), *Signification and Significance* by Charles Morris (1964), *The Language of Logic* by Morton Schagin (1968), and *Towards a Semantic Description of English* by Geoffrey N. Leech (1970).

INTERPRETIVE SEMANTICS:

When Noam Chomsky presented his revolutionary grammar in his 1957 *Syntactic Structures,* he did not pay particular attention to meaning or semantics. It wasn't until 1963, that someone proposed a way to work with semantics as part of generative grammar. Jerrold J. Katz and Jerry Fodor, both philosophers at MIT, published an article in *Language* entitled, "The Structure of Semantic Theory." The semantic model outlined in this article was further developed in a book entitled *An Integrated Theory of Linguistic Descriptions* (1964) by Katz and Paul Postal, a linguist. The article in *Language* and the book by Katz and Postal were responsible for many of the revisions of the generative-transformational model which were proposed by Chomsky in his *Aspects of the Theory of Syntax* (1965).

Interpretive semantics, now also called the standard theory, relies on projection rules to give an interpretation to a sentence. According to this model, each lexical item has associated with it a certain number of features. One of these features is the part of speech which is partially determined by the strict subcategorization constraints on a particular item. For example, any particular verb characteristically requires certain grammatical categories to precede it and follow it. Thus, an intransitive verb such as *walk* does not require anything to go with it except a subject, while a transitive verb such as *hit* requires both a subject and a direct object. A verb like *dart* must be followed by an adverb of motion. These are statements about the strict subcategorization of these three verbs. In sentences like "John hit," or "John saw of" the strict subcategorization requirements of the verb are violated, in the first sentence by not having anything after the transitive verb, and in the second sentence by having a preposition after the transitive verb rather than the appropriate noun phrase.

Subcategorization rules are basically concerned with syntactic matters rather than semantic matters. But there are also certain semantic features associated with each lexical item. The semantic markers are those semantic features which have general importance in the grammar. A particular semantic marker will be a feature of not just a single word, but of many words. Semantic distinguishers have relevance for only a particular word. A distinguisher is the semantic feature which separates one lexical item from all others. For example, in the most common meaning of the word "bachelor," the feature "noun" is the part of speech: the features "human," "male," and "adult," are the semantic markers, and "never-married" is the distinguisher.

It is the function of the projection rules to scan the features, i.e., the part of speech, the semantic markers, and the distinguishers of each lexical item, and to combine these features with those of other lexical items with which the individual words form a constituent, and to determine which of the features are compatible with each other at a particular level. Thus, the projection rules would show that the word "ball" is ambiguous, meaning either a spherical object for use in a game, or a formal dance. But the projection rules would show that the expression "soccer ball" is unambiguous since the features of "soccer" are normally compatible only with the spherical-object meaning of "ball," rather than the formal dance meaning. Projection rules can therefore be seen as rules of disambiguation. After the projection rules have scanned the entire sentence, including embedded sentences, if any, in much the same way as they scanned the features of the expression "soccer ball," they would be able to specify if a sentence is deviant or has no composite meaning, i.e., is anomalous, or if it has one composite meaning, i.e., is unique, or if it has more than one composite meaning, i.e., is ambiguous. By making a distinction between the syntactic features and the semantic features, it is also possible to tell if an anomalous or ambiguous sentence is deviant because of syntax or semantics. For example, the sentence, "He was seated by the President," is semantically ambiguous because the confusion is due to the double meaning of *by*. The sentence, "I won't speak at any more dull women's meetings," is syntactically ambiguous because the confusion is due to the placement of the two modifiers *dull* and *women* in front of *meetings*. The syntax does not show which word *dull* is modifying.

The important differences between Chomsky 1957 and Chomsky 1965 result from the attempt to incorporate the semantic theory of Katz, Fodor, and Postal into the transformational model. One important difference is that the 1965 model makes frequent reference to the cover term, Complex Symbol or CS, which refers to all of the features of a particular lexical item. Chomsky did not actually write semantic rules into his revised grammar, but by using CS as his last notation on tree diagrams, he made it possible for semantic information to be plugged into his syntactic analysis. Another difference is that in the later model the tree diagram shows sentences to be embedded into other sentences in the following manner:

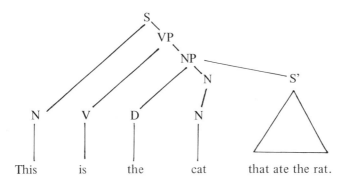

Before the 1965 *Aspects,* generative transformationalists made a distinction between kernel sentences, which are the most basic simple sentences, and derived sentences, which have been changed into such things as questions, imperatives, passives, and negatives. They also generated each sentence separately and then combined the sentences together by means of a generalized transformation such as the following:

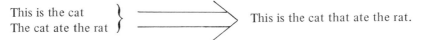

There were problems in applying projection rules in this earlier model because each sentence had to be scanned separately. This meant that the projection rules could not be used to determine the meaning of the super sentence that resulted when the two sentences were merged together in some way.

Further reading on these matters might be found in Roderick A. Jacobs and Peter S. Rosenbaum's *English Transformational Grammar* (1968), Jerrold J. Katz's *Semantic Theory* (1972), and Ray S. Jackendoff's *Semantic Interpretation in Generative Grammar* (1972).

GENERATIVE SEMANTICS:

In recent works by such linguists as George Lakoff, James McCawley, Jeffrey Gruber, and Leonhard Lipka, a number of problems in the interpretive semantics model have been noted. These writers reject the idea that syntax should be the grammatical base. First, they say that syntax occupies an intermediate position between phonology and semantics. When using syntax as the base, it is therefore necessary to go in two different directions, up to the phonology and down to the semantics. Secondly, semantic features are universal whereas syntax and phonology are mainly language specific. They claim that it makes more sense to go from this universal base toward the more specific and divergent syntactic and phonological components of various particular languages. Third, they feel that there may not be any justification for a separate syntactic level at all, and if there is no independently justified level of syntax, then this level cannot be the base level since it doesn't really exist. And fourth, as Wallace Chafe has pointed out, the speech act—and probably the origin of language as well—begins with concepts and these are encoded into language rather than the reverse being true. A final criticism of the interpretive semantic model is that it has two separate kinds of rules—transformations for handling syntactic and phonological matters, and projection rules for handling semantic matters. The generative semanticists feel that only one type of rule is necessary and this is the transformation. They feel that they can handle semantic information by postulating higher predicates and predicate-lifting transformations which have the effect of combining a lower predicate with a higher predicate which results in a new word with all of the meanings of the two words from which it was formed. For example, they see the verb *kill* as consisting of the state *dead* plus the two higher level predicates *cause* and *become.* Thus, taking the expression, "cause to become dead" one predicate-lifting transformation will change *become dead* into *die,* and a second will change *cause to die* into *kill.* It has been argued by non-generative semanticists that *cause to die* does not mean exactly the same as *kill.* The generative semanticists have answered that the higher predicate *cause* is different from the lexical item *cause,* and in fact differs in exactly those ways which make *cause to die* an accurate paraphrase of *kill.* In a way it appears that on this particular point the generative semanticists have come full cycle in their reasoning. They claim to be able to handle semantics without resorting to semantic features. Yet what they call their higher predicates look very much like semantic features since they make a distinction between them and regular lexical units or words.

Some of the best readings on the generative semantics viewpoint are James D. McCawley's "Where do Noun Phrases Come From?" In *Readings in English Transformational Grammar* (1970), Jeffrey Gruber's *Studies in Lexical Relations* (1970), Paul Postal's "On the Surface Verb 'remind' " in *Linguistic Inquiry* (1970), George Lakoff's "On Generative Semantics" in *Semantics: An Interdisciplinary Reader in Philosophy, Linguistics, and Psychology* (1971), and Leonhard Lipka's *Semantic Structure and Word Formation* (1972).

CASE GRAMMAR:

Shortly after *Aspects* was published in 1965, Charles Fillmore began working on a new kind of semantically oriented grammar. For more than a year mimeographed copies of his article outlining this model were circulated among linguists. Finally in 1968, the article entitled "The Case for Case," was published in *Universals in Linguistic Theory* edited by Emmon Bach and Robert Harmes. In this article, Fillmore proposed that all languages have deep cases like Agent, Instrument, Experiencer, Object, etc. (These will be capitalized to distinguish them from the standard parts of speech, some of which have the same name.) He defined the Agent as the animate actor, the Instrument as the inanimate cause, the Experiencer (this term was suggested in his later work) as the animate receiver, the Object as the thing manipulated, etc. And although he took note of a correlation between subjects and Agents, between direct objects and Objects, between indirect objects and Experiencers, etc., he pointed out that this correlation is by no means perfect since subject, direct object, and indirect object are surface structure designations, while Agent, Object, and Experiencer are deep structure designations. Thus, to use his example, the Agent is a subject in "John broke the window with a hammer"; the Instrument is a subject in "A hammer broke the window"; and the Object is a subject in "The window broke." In showing that there is a partial correlation between the surface structure functions and deep structure cases, Fillmore noted that whenever there is an Agent in an active English sentence it is automatically the subject of the sentence; the Instrument is next in line of eligibility as a subject, and the Object is eligible to become the subject only if there is no Agent or Instrument in the sentence.

Fillmore generalized that each deep case has a particular preposition associated with it. For example, the preposition for the Agent case is *by* as in "Paris was captured *by* the German army." The preposition for the Experiencer case is *to* as in "John told a story *to* Mary." The preposition for the Instrumental case is *with* as in "John hit the window *with* a hammer." And the preposition for the Object case is also *with* as in "John loaded the truck *with* hay." He feels that the preposition is always present in the deep structure, but is lost whenever the noun phrase becomes a subject, a direct object, or an indirect object in a surface structure, as in "B̶y̶ the German army captured Paris," "John told t̶o̶ Mary a story," "W̶i̶t̶h̶ a hammer hit the window," and "John loaded w̶i̶t̶h̶ hay onto the truck," respectively. In the deep case, Fillmore considers all noun phrases to be prepositional phrases. He pointed out that the noun phrases can be moved around in the sentence or be deleted as long as the preposition remains with it, but as soon as the preposition is lost, as it is when the noun phrase becomes a subject or direct object, the noun phrase can no longer be moved or deleted.

To this point, we have been discussing Fillmore's treatment of noun phrases. He handles verbs not in terms of deep cases, but rather in terms of deep case frames. That is, he would classify verbs according to which deep cases they co-occur with. In the sentence "John jumped from one side of the ditch to the other side," the verb *jump* has associated with it an Agent (John), a Source (one side of the ditch), and a Goal (the other side of the ditch). The fact that the sentence, "John jumped," is grammatical in English while the sentence, "Jumped," is not grammatical, shows that for the verb *jump* an Agent is necessary, whereas a Source and a Goal are possible, but not necessary. Fillmore would therefore say that the verb *jump* has the case frame [+− A (S) (G)]. In reading this kind of notation of case frames, the brackets indicate that the enclosed cases are members of the set of cases that occur with a particular verb. The plus sign means that the cases mentioned are present rather than absent. The blank space stands for the position that the verb would fill if it were there. This blank space can be read as "in the context of." Next Fillmore lists the cases which go with the verb. In actual use, at least in English, one of these cases will precede the verb because it will be acting as subject. In the sentence, "John enjoyed the movie," both the Experiencer (John) and the Object (the movie) are necessary; this verb therefore has the case frame [+− E O]. As another example, consider the sentence, "John hit the wall (with a hammer)." In this sentence, the Agent (John), and the Object (the wall) are necessary to the sentence, but the Instrument (a hammer) is not necessary. The verb *hit* therefore has the case frame [+− A (I) O]. A very important consequence of this type of analysis is that a classification of verbs according to their case frames corresponds very closely to a classification of verbs according to their real-world significance. Thus, the case frame [+− E O] is appropriate not only for the verb *enjoy,* but for all verbs of psychological events. And the case frame [+ A (I) O] is appropriate not only for *hit,* but for all verbs of contact. And even more exciting is the possibility that [+− E O] is appropriate not only for verbs of psychological events in English, but for verbs of psychological events in *all* human languages. Because Fillmore is dealing with universal concepts, he cautions that the cases are unordered in these case frames, although it may be decided later that ordering is necessary so as to represent eligibility for such things as subject marking if this is shown to be a universal hierarchy.

Two important criticisms have been directed at the case model. The first question is whether deep cases are adequate as a universal linguistic base. The second question is related to the first; if it is shown that something more basic than deep cases, such as semantic features, is required as a universal linguistic base, then can deep cases be justified as an intermediate structure somewhere between deep structure and surface structure? Our own feeling is that although deep cases provide some very important insights into the workings of language, they are too gross to be semantic primes. Therefore we would make only the weaker claim that they represent an intermediate structure. And even with this claim, further work may show that semantic features by themselves are perfectly adequate and possibly even simpler than deep cases in explaining the fascinating facts which Fillmore brought to light.

In addition to his statements regarding deep cases and case frames, Fillmore made a number of important observations about what the generative semanticists call predicate raising. Fillmore handled such information by entailment rules in a kind of hierarchy, whereby *require* would be said to entail *permit; certain* to entail *possible; steal* and *accuse* to entail both *criticize* and *responsible,* etc. He would say that *persuade* entails *cause* and *believe,* while the generative semanticists would postulate these expressions as lower predicates. Fillmore is also very interested in figuring out presupposition, i.e., what a speaker assumes to be true and known before he says anything. For example, in the sentence, "Harry realizes that John is President," it is presupposed that "John is President." Since negation does not affect presupposition, the sentence "Harry doesn't realize that John is President," also presupposes that "John is President." One aspect of presupposition which Fillmore is especially interested in is that resulting from various kinds of orientation. A cube in space has six sides. If this cube is sitting on the ground, it has a top, a bottom, and four sides. If in addition, one side is more ornate than the others, it has a top, a bottom, a front, a back and two sides. And finally, if there is some reason to distinguish one side from the other, it has a top, a bottom, a front, a back, a right side, and a left side. A dresser would be an example of this last situation, and it would be noteworthy that the right-hand side of a dresser is the same as the right-hand side of the person who is facing the dresser, rather than the right side of the dresser itself. Fillmore has been very concerned with such aspects of language, although it is not entirely clear how this fits into his Case Model grammar.

In this Case Model grammar Fillmore has been basically interested in justifying his deep cases by morphological and syntactic considerations. He uses several tests for deciding on the membership of a case. One such test is based on the assumption that only members of the same case can be conjoined. For example, with the acceptable "John and Mary broke the window," there are two Agents joined as the subject. But the sentence, *"John and a hammer broke the window," is deviant because an Agent and an Instrument have been joined. Another test Fillmore uses is that there can be only a single use of a deep case per simple predicate. For example, "John broke the window with a hammer," is acceptable, but *"The hammer broke the window with a chisel," is unacceptable because of the two different uses of the Instrument case. Fillmore's third test for case membership has already been mentioned. It is the particular preposition used as a marker, i.e., *John* is an Agent in the sentence, "The cookie was stolen by John," because *John* can be marked with the preposition *by*. *By* is still the marker in the deep structure of "John stole the cookie," but it has been deleted from the surface structure as happens when an Agent noun phrase becomes the subject of the sentence.

Some of the followers of Fillmore have not placed such a heavy reliance on syntactic and morphological considerations for determining deep cases. Although they have not contested Fillmore's syntactic and morphological tests, they have supplemented these tests with semantic evidence stated in terms of semantic features. Their work can be seen in Dorothy Mack Lambert's dissertation, "The Semantic Syntax of Metaphor" (1969), Ana Maria McCoy's dissertation, "A Case Grammar Classification of Spanish Verbs" (1969), and Thomas Shroyer's dissertation, "An Investigation of the Semantics of English as a Proposed Basis for Language Curriculum Materials" (1969).

Two books based on the case model are John M. Anderson's *The Grammar of Case: Toward a Localistic Theory* (1971) and D. Terence Langendoen's *Essentials of English Grammar* (1970).

Wallace Chafe in his *Meaning and the Structure of Language* (1970) states that "When introspection and surface evidence are contradictory, it is the former which is decisive," (page 122). His model of grammar differs from Fillmore's in that it gives priority in assigning cases to semantic categories rather than to syntactic or morphological considerations. Chafe has a lengthy discussion of various kinds of semantic features: derivational, inflectional, and selectional. Chafe also postulates a direct relationship between case frames and semantic categories of verbs such as state, process, event, and action. He indicates that a state is a one-place predicate which is filled by a Patient (what Fillmore calls an Object) as in "The wood is dry." He considers a process to be a change of state which is also a one-place predicate with a Patient filling that one place as in "The wood dried." He considers an action also to be a one-place predicate with the one place being filled by an Agent as in "Michael ran." An event is a combination of an action and a process. Thus Chafe would conceive of the sentence, "Michael dried the wood," as an event consisting of an action (Michael acted) and a process (the wood dried). Since an event consists of an action, which has an Agent, and a process, which has a Patient, it is logical that an event such as "Michael dried the wood," would be considered a two-place predicate consisting of an Agent (Michael), and a Patient (the wood).

It can be seen from the above examples that Chafe's grammar makes use of deep cases. Unlike Fillmore, however, Chafe marks these deep cases as being hierarchical. For example in the sentence, "John made Bill a tie clasp," Fillmore would consider the Agent (John), the Benefactive (Bill), and the Object (a tie clasp) all to be on the same level. But Chafe would diagram this sentence as follows so that it would show the subject-predicate dichotomy:

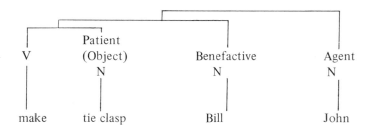

Chafe's diagramming tends to superordinate those cases likely to become subjects and to subordinate the others.

Chafe is also very interested in discourse analysis, i.e., the grammar of items larger than the sentence. He points out, for example, that such a sentence as "I bought a car yesterday, but the fender was bashed in," is not ungrammatical, even though the definite article *the* is marking a previously unidentified noun. His point is that when a speaker introduces a concept like *car* he is at the same time introducing all of the parts that one assumes are automatically a part of all (or most) cars. When someone mentions a car, it can be assumed that the hearer has conceptualized a car in his mind with many of its parts, and it is therefore possible to refer to *the* windshield, *the* tires, *the* hand brake, etc. even though the windshield, tires, and hand brake have not been previously designated independently. This observation has important ramifications in considering the nature of semantic features.

One of the most important considerations in discourse analysis is the pronoun system. Postal and others have shown that pronouns have both deep structure and surface structure constraints. Relative pronouns, personal pronouns, and reflexive pronouns must all have antecedents, but Paul Postal has pointed out that identity of sense is a necessary but not a sufficient condition to allow pronominalization. Identity of reference is also required. The sentence, "Max's parents are dead and he deeply misses them," is grammatical because the two noun phrases *parents* and *them* have both identity of sense and identity of reference. However, the sentence *"Max is an orphan, and he deeply misses them," is ungrammatical because the two noun phrases *orphan* and *them* have identity of sense in that *orphan* means a person without parents and *them* refers to this incorporated term *parents,* but they do not have identity of reference in that *orphan* and *them* do not refer to exactly the same thing. Stated differently, Postal has shown that a feature must reach the surface structure in order to be pronominalized.

IV. Anomaly, Ambiguity, and Discourse

This chapter will briefly discuss three different areas which are open to semantic analysis: first will be deviation or anomaly; second will be ambiguity; and third will be units of communication larger than a sentence but still related in some way.

ANOMALY:

Many of the features of the deep structure of languages are universal. But it is obvious that surface structure, i.e., the actual sounds and their linear arrangements are largely language dependent and idiosyncratic. This is because there are numerous constraints on the ordering of sounds, the ordering of words, and on transformations. These constraints vary from language to language. Some linguists in fact feel that the basic function of transformations is to specify the constraints which hold in a particular language.

Usually these constraints are not violated, at least in formal writing, and the resultant sentences are perfectly well formed. Such sentences are said to be both grammatical and acceptable. There are many ways, however, that these constraints can be violated, and the result is a sentence which, although not meaningless, is ungrammatical or unacceptable. Sentences like this are called anomalous. To get a better understanding of what is meant by anomaly, we will look at a number of violations and rank them according to degree of anomaly beginning with the most anomalous type of sentence and going by stages to a perfectly normal and acceptable sentence.

The most anomalous type of structure is a random group of words arranged in random order, for example, *"Retaliation dog damn swim a." Even this sentence is somewhat structured since all of the words are normal English words. And it is difficult to say unequivocally that the sentence is meaningless because one of the unusual powers of the human brain is to provide a logical and reasonable reading even for random groups of words like the one above.

A slightly less anomalous sentence is one in which the words are selected and only the ordering is random, for example, *"Room boy little the into darted a." This sentence could be unscrambled to become, "A little boy darted into the room," but as it stands it is severely anomalous and would strain the imagination of a person attempting to provide a meaningful interpretation and/or a meaningful context.

The rest of our examples will contain English words in a basically acceptable English syntactic pattern, but each will illustrate the violation of a different type of constraint. A sentence like, *"A little boy darted," for example, is ungrammatical because the verb *darted* requires some sort of complement like "into the room." A necessary category is missing. If the slot were filled by a word from the wrong category, as in *"A little boy darted the bicycle," the sentence would still be anomalous.

A less severe type of violation would occur if a word were taken from the correct category, but the wrong subcategory, for example, *"He moved both furnitures into the other room." Here the word *furnitures* is a noun, and it is filling a slot that requires a noun, yet the sentence is ungrammatical since *furniture* is a mass noun in English and can not be made plural. As we learn more about a particular language, our constraints become more sophisticated and less general. A sentence like, *"Hope frightened sincerity," is ungrammatical because the word *frightened* must have a concrete noun as its subject and an animate noun as its object. Deviations of this type are called violations of "strict subcategorization."

When a sentence is anomalous because of the positioning of the words it is described as being syntactically anomalous. But such a sentence as Chomsky's famous, "Colorless green ideas sleep furiously," is semantically rather than syntactically anomalous. The markings on the words which help to identify their parts of speech and the way they are positioned, make the sentence appear entirely grammatical in the same pattern as, "Thoughtless young men behave rashly," but there are many semantic incompatibilities. Something which is *green* cannot at the same time be *colorless,* and ideas are not usually identified as either with or without color. Furthermore, *ideas* don't *sleep,* and sleeping is too passive an act to be done *furiously.*

Another type of anomaly is lack of truth. The sentence, "Iranians speak Italian," is syntactically and semantically well formed, but it is not true. More complicated to explain is the sentence, "John didn't realize that Iranians speak Italian." This is syntactically and semantically well formed and true, but it is misleading. It presupposes something which is false, and therefore violates what some linguists call the *happiness* or *felicity* conditions.

There are other anomalous sentences which are true and are syntactically and semantically well formed without violating happiness conditions, for example, "The bus driver ran the girl who was crossing the street on her yellow bicycle which was not equipped with brakes *down.*" Such a sentence would never occur because there is too much linguistic material intervening between the parts of the two-word verb *ran down.* From the point of view of competence (a theoretical matter) the sentence is fine, but from the point of view of potential performance (a practical matter) the sentence is ill formed.

Other types of anomaly would include words spoken with a foreign accent such as "He's sipping [rather than zipping] up his coat." Similar to this are regional variations like, "Y'all stay a spell, hear?", and social variations like, "He don't deserve no better." The following chart illustrates thirteen degrees of anomaly. This is not a set number nor a complete representation, but it is useful in suggesting different types of anomaly and showing that some types are more severe, more deviant from the norm, than are other types:

DEGREES OF ANOMALY

RANK:	EXAMPLE:	DESCRIPTION OF ANOMALY:
1.	Retaliation dog damn swim a.	Random words: random order
2.	Room boy little the into darted a.	Selected words: random order
3.	A little boy darted a bicycle.	Wrong category
4.	A little boy darted.	Missing category
5.	He moved both furnitures into the other room.	Wrong high level subcategory
6.	Hope frightened sincerity.	Wrong low level subcategory
7.	Colorless green ideas sleep furiously.	Semantic incompatibility
8.	Iranians speak Italian.	Untruth
9.	John didn't realize that Iranians speak Italian.	Misleading
10.	The bus driver ran the girl who was crossing the street on her yellow bicycle which was not equipped with brakes down.	Unacceptable, awkward
11.	He's sipping up his coat.	Foreign accent
12.	He don't deserve no better.	Social dialect
13.	Y'all stay a spell, hear?	Regional dialect

The next step would be a non anomalous, well-formed sentence such as, "Iranians speak Farsi."

Semantic theory is still a young science. As we come to know more and more about semantics, our judgments about degrees of anomaly will probably become more specific and more valid. A number of facts seem to be relevant, with the most basic being that *anomalous* and *meaningless* must not be equated. All of these sentences have meaning. In fact, in one sense, the more deviant a sentence is, the more meaningful it is, since it then becomes open to a wider range of possible interpretations. The number and type of constraint violations are also relevant in determining the degree of anomaly; and in terms of semantic incompatibilities, it is not enough to say that two words are incompatible without specifying the nature of the incompatibility in terms of semantic features.

AMBIGUITY:

Contrary to popular belief ambiguity (which occurs much more often than most people realize) is not always accidental but is often the result of very careful planning. A great deal of our humor is based on ambiguity, and advertisers frequently use puns to attract attention to their product. The most common kind of pun centers around double meanings in homonyms. For example a sale on new kitchen appliances such as mixers, can openers, and coffee percolators was advertised as a "Counter Revolution." Shatterproof glasses were advertised as "Good to the last drop," and decorated paper towels were advertised as "A pretty, tough towel."

Sometimes puns are made on two different words that are similar in sound. The effect is refreshing because the actual meaning is first seen and then when the sentence is said out loud the double meaning or the relationship to an old familiar saying comes as an added bonus. The American Tuberculosis Association's slogan, "It's a matter of life and breath," is effective because it triggers the listener to think of the old phrase *life and death.* "Every litter bit hurts," makes us think of *every little bit,* and the General Electric advertisement for "Softglow lights, they couldn't glare less," makes us think of *couldn't care less."* The ambiguity in these examples exists not because of actual homonyms, but become of a close phonological relationship to set phrases which are familiar to the listener.

Another kind of intentional ambiguity is that which occurs in literature through symbolism. Satire, sarcasm, allusion, simile, and metaphor are possible only because the human mind can cope with ambiguity. We enjoy reading something and probing for a second, a third, or even a fourth level of meaning. It is partially because we need time for this kind of thinking and probing that it takes us longer to read the same number of words in poetry and great literature than in the daily newspaper. When we are hurrying to communicate everyday information, we do not want to be bothered with ambiguity. This desire to avoid ambiguity and therefore misunderstanding in objective business like communication has led to the development of the attitude that ambiguity is a negative quality. But rather than thinking that ambiguity is something to be avoided, it would be better to think of it as something to be understood and controlled.

A good book treating the subject of ambiguity is Jan Kooij's *Ambiguity in Natural Language: An Investigation of Certain Problems in its Linguistic Description* (1971). In this book the author makes the point that there is a difference between ambiguity and vagueness. When something is ambiguous there are two or more distinct interpretations that are possible. But when something is vague, the listener or reader does not think of any definite interpretation, but rather is unsure or confused as to just what was meant. Vagueness, to some degree exists in practically all communication. Ambiguity is less common but is still present in a surprisingly large part of our daily communication.

Lexical ambiguity, which is what most people think of when they hear the term *ambiguity,* is only one of the thirteen types which Kooij discusses in his book. Several types of ambiguity could be resolved by careful speech, i.e., stresses and pauses and intonation, but this is frequently not done because the speaker has only one thought in mind and therefore isn't aware of how he should make his statement sound in order to cancel out a meaning which might occur to one of his listeners. For example if a speaker realized that in the following sentence *failing* could be interpreted as either the main verb of the sentence or as an adjective, he could show the intended meaning through stress: "Some members of our faculty are failing graduate students." A pause after *monkey* would probably clear up the ambiguity in, "A lady carrying a monkey and a large elephant entered the circus tent." And pitch, stress, and pausing would all point to the intended meaning in, "Chapman reports open seminar," where the main verb could be either *reports* or *open.*

A particularly troublesome kind of ambiguity which is solved by neither punctuation in writing nor stress patterns in speech is that of unclear modification. For example, is the sentence, "The men were both tall and husky," talking about two men or about an unspecified number of men who had the two qualities mentioned? In, "We were excluding totally unconditioned athletes," is *totally* modifying *excluding* or *unconditioned?* In "Mr. Santi refuses to speak at any more dull women's meetings," is *dull* modifying *meetings* or *women?* And in, "I was surprised to find out that she could telephone her husband in prison," is she in prison or is her husband in prison?

When two prepositional phrases are used next to each other, it is hard to tell how much of the sentence is included in the domain of the last phrase. For example, does the school or the library have a fine reputation in, "She has applied to work in a library at a school which has a fine reputation."?

Sometimes it is hard to tell whether something is the deep-subject or object in a sentence. The most famous example of this kind of ambiguity is, "The shooting of the hunters frightened me." Here we don't know whether the hunters were doing the shooting or were being shot. In "The little boy is too young to understand," we don't know whether someone is trying to understand the little boy or the little boy is trying to understand something or someone. In, "Police closed in when they heard the booing of the demonstrators," we don't know whether the demonstrators were booing or were being booed. And in "The lawyer claimed that the constant scrubbing of the maids was an invasion of privacy," we don't know whether the maids kept scrubbing the lawyer's office or whether someone kept scrubbing the maids, or if the maids were being kept off the team.

There are certain verbs such as *call, name,* and *appoint* which can take two complements. One of these is always a direct object. It is hard to tell if the other one is being used as an indirect object or objective complement. For example, "Congressman Smith appointed his brother an assistant," can mean either that Congressman Smith appointed his brother to be an assistant or he appointed someone to be an assistant to his brother. This is the type of ambiguity in the joke where someone says, "Call me a taxi," and someone else says, "Okay, you're a taxi."

Since comparisons are seldom stated in their complete form, they lend themselves to ambiguity because the listener must imagine which of two or more ways to end the comparison. For example, "Dan really thought he deserved more in life than Susan," could mean that Dan thought he deserved more than Susan deserved or he deserved someone better than Susan for a wife. This same kind of double meaning is in, "Janice liked Homer as much as Jerry," and in, "Being an old hand at blind dates, Stan expected something less than Miss America."

Adverbs of frequency can sometimes be confused with adverbs of manner. The normal position for an adverb of frequency is between the subject and the verb, while the normal position for an adverb of manner is at the end of the sentence. This means that when a speaker puts an adverb of frequency at the end of the sentence it is sometimes confused with an adverb of manner as in, "She doesn't swim the butterfly stroke normally," or "He broils steak rarely."

Indefinite pronouns can be confusing simply because they are so indefinite. "There was one pitcher and one glass for everyone in the airport," can mean that each person in the airport had a pitcher and a glass or that there was one to be shared by everyone. "All of us had a room," doesn't tell whether we all had a room together or separately, nor does, "Everybody came in a car," indicate whether people came together or separately.

Knowing whether a particular word or phrase is functioning as an adjective or adverb would clear up the ambiguity in these sentences: "You can take the big one upstairs," and "Can you lift that child over there?"

Negative statements become complicated when reason clauses are added to them. For example, "She didn't stay home from the party because of the entertainment," could mean either that she stayed home from the party but it had nothing to do with the entertainment, or that she went to the party because of the entertainment. This same type of ambiguity appears in:

The governor announced that there would be no changes in policy because
   of the new commissioner.
The meeting was not called due to the airline strike.
She seldom comes because of social pressure.

The above types of ambiguity have been recognized and discussed by grammarians for many years. More recent research has centered around such things as ambiguous tense. In English it is a very common practice to delete words changing clauses into phrases or single words; this affects the appearance of tense. For example the tense in the dependent clause is clearly past in the sentence, "I shook hands with the person who was the President." But when this is shortened to, "I shook hands with the President," we don't know whether the President referred to is the present President, a former President, or even a President who has been elected but not yet inaugurated. English is full of terms of reference which exhibit an imprecision of real-world time. For example, the sentence, "On our first date, my wife and I went bowling," is an imprecision because at the time of the speaker's first date, the girl he was with was not yet his wife. Another example is, "In 1959 our oldest son was born." The child may now be the couple's oldest son, but in 1959 he was their only son, not their oldest son. In trying to analyze this kind of problem, grammarians make a distinction between true tense which is the time of the recounted event in the past and narrative tense which is the time of the speech act. The ambiguity is resolved only when the listener can correctly sort out these two tenses.

Some words have a durative quality while synonyms of them have a punctual or short-term quality. When these words are interchanged a kind of ambiguity can result. For example, *attend* is a durative but *go to* is not. If someone asks, "Did you attend college?, on grammatical grounds a straight answer is needed, but if someone asks, "Did you go to college," the answer can be the joke, "Oh yes, I went in one door and out the other." It is because of this ambiguity of duration that Mark Twain was able to say that he'd quit smoking dozens of times.

The intent of a sentence is also part of ambiguity. In "He cut his finger," the action could be either intentional or accidental. The statement, "He killed himself," has the same ambiguity as compared to the alternate phrase clearly showing intent, "He committed suicide."

Another ambiguous area relates to possessive nouns. The question is, in what sense is something possessed. Does *Sanford's book* mean that Sanford bought, stole, borrowed, wrote, published, designed, illustrated, edited, or printed the book? The question of just what is being asserted is also an ambiguous area. This will be talked about more under discourse analysis. But what it relates to is the presupposition behind a sentence. English stress patterns can bring almost any part of a sentence to the listener's attention. But in writing, the phonological element is not present so a variety of interpretations are possible.

All of these problems which have been mentioned are just a brief sampling. Vagueness and ambiguity in language is the rule rather than the exception. Practically any sentence when viewed out of context has numerous interpretations and can become unique only through context in which the semantic components of a particular sentence must jibe with all of the other semantic components in the linguistic situation as well as in the real world known by the listener.

THE DISCOURSE: GOING BEYOND THE SENTENCE:

A discourse, whether it is a sentence, a paragraph, a chapter, a book, a series of books, or whatever, has a great deal of unity, coherence, and logical progression. Just as there are semantic constraints within the sentence, there are semantic constraints for the discourse. These are mostly language-independent, which means they are universal. For example, every discourse must have a purpose. The group of words, "John has a house," is perfectly acceptable as a sentence but is not very successful as a discourse because it lacks purpose. "John built a very large house," or "John built a mansion," are better as discourses because they provide us with interesting information by helping to characterize John either as a wealthy person or as a person willing to go into debt.

It is the purpose of the discourse that largely determines the use of performatives. The purpose of a particular discourse might be to gain information, in which case there will be various types of questions, or it may be to get something done, in which case there will be various types of commands. If the purpose is to convey information, there will be mainly declarative statements and possibly rhetorical questions. If the purpose is to christen a ship or marry a couple, the form will be highly ritualized. If the purpose is to create a false impression, there will be a relationship to the real world in only a very vague or misleading way. Obviously, there are a great many different purposes for discourses, but the important point is that each discourse must have a purpose or else it is not a discourse.

In any discourse there is a certain relationship between the speaker and the listener. This is greatly influenced by the amount of information they share. If the speaker and listener are husband and wife, they probably share a great deal of information and a great many attitudes and can therefore communicate with a much smaller discourse than average. If the speaker and listener are unrelated members of the same ethnic group, then they probably share more information than if they are members of different ethnic groups. And even two people with opposite interests, opposite values, and opposite experiential backgrounds, still share a great many things with each other just by the fact that they inhabit the same planet.

In a discourse the concept of authority is also important. A person cannot perform a marriage ceremony unless he has the authority to do so. Usually a person doesn't command someone to do something unless he is in a position to have some control over the other person's actions and unless the other person is able and willing to follow the command. Normally we don't ask information from a person unless we expect that person to have the information we need. The whole idea of verbal "put-downs" as described in Eric Berne's popular book *The Games People Play* is relevant to the establishment of the speaker-listener relationship.

All of this points to the fact that certain things about the speaker-listener relationship and the community as a whole must be taken into consideration in a discourse. However, a great deal more than this is signalled in a discourse where, for example, there are often clues about the geographical and social dialects of the speakers. The style of a discourse may be formal or informal, and from a language standpoint it may be very conservative filled with set phrases and euphemisms or it may be linguistically radical filled with unusual constructions and direct references to taboo areas. The sentence structure might be shortened and terse, normal, or very complex. The discourse may be full of redundancies or very succinct. Parts of it might be appropriate or inappropriate to the subject matter and to the situation in which the information is recounted. There are a great many ways to vary the style of a discourse, but usually, a particular discourse is stylistically consistent throughout.

Another feature of a discourse is its element of organization. A discourse can be organized according to such things as time, space, generality, importance, or cause. Since human language can be divorced from the real world in time and space, it becomes necessary to establish the time and place somewhere in the discourse by means of what are generally called adverbials. Time, which is a fact of the real world, differs from tense, which is a grammatical phenomenon. For example, the verb in the sentence, "John plays basketball," is in the simple present tense form, but it does not represent the present time. Instead it represents past, present, and future times. The sentence that would represent the present time would have the form of the present progressive: "John is playing basketball." Unlike

English, in many languages it is not necessary for each verb to have a tense. In these languages there is a closer relationship between the linguistic time, established in adverbials, and real-world time. Also there is less redundancy of grammatical marking in respect to time.

Any discourse is assumed by the listener to have some sort of organization. For example, if the two unrelated sentences, "John broke his arm," and "Jim knows an important man in Detroit," are spaced next to each other in a two-sentence discourse, the listener will strain to see a relationship between the two sentences. He may assume that the important man that Jim knows in Detroit is a medical doctor and could therefore fix John's broken arm, or that the man in Detroit is a philanthropist who might pay to have Jim's arm fixed, or that the man in Detroit might be the coach of a football team that Jim plays for, or any other number of possible relationships. If the listener cannot figure out a relationship, or if what he thinks of is vague, or ambiguous, or misleading, he may very well say something like, "Come again!" or "What does that have to do with it?", which is his way of saying that the discourse is unacceptable because there is no obviously unique relationship between the two sentences and it is the responsibility of the speaker to provide such a relationship. If the two sentences placed next to each other were "John broke his arm," and "He was benched during the entire tournament," then an organization becomes apparent because there is both a temporal and a causal relationship between the first and the second sentence. We assume, though it is certainly not stated anywhere, that John's breaking his arm not only preceded, but in fact was the cause of, his being benched during the tournament. Notice that the order of these two sentences is not random, as can be seen by comparing the two sentences juxtaposed in reverse order: "John was benched during the entire game. He broke his arm." Although this order may be possible, it is not as likely. If the sentences did appear like this it might be that the latter sentence was added as an afterthought or as an explanation given in response to a questioning or surprised look from the listener. In general it is assumed that the sequential ordering of the sentences in a discourse reveals the sequential ordering of the events being talked about.

In our example, there is not only a chronological ordering signaled, but also a cause-and-effect relationship. Of course, chronology and cause-and-effect are not totally unrelated. In general a cause happens before, at least not after, its effect. The same types of assumptions as relate time to causality, can also relate time and space, as in the following mini-discourse:

> Mary bought a bracelet in Payson; she wore it through Spanish Fork and Springville; but in Salt Lake she discovered that the bracelet was no longer on her wrist.

Again without any overt markers, there is a chronological ordering signaled. We assume that she bought the bracelet first, she wore it second, and she lost it third, partially because this is the sequencing of the sentences as they appear in the discourse and partially because of what we know about the words *buy, wore,* and *lose.* A person cannot wear something or lose something unless she has first gained possession of that thing. And whereas she must gain possession of the bracelet before she wears it, she probably loses it after wearing it because if she lost it first she would have had no opportunity to wear it and that would not have been part of the discourse.

Such facts as these may be considered too obvious to deserve mention, but the point is that this is the kind of logical reasoning that people involved in a discourse go through in order for the organization of a discourse to be established. We do not mean to imply that discourse is organized without overt signals. On the contrary, there are many overt signals in a discourse, but even when these are missing, the discourse is organized in some way, and this organization contributes greatly to the meaning conveyed. This is one of the reasons that a sentence in context is so much more meaningful than the same sentence out of context.

Because two sentences juxtaposed in a discourse share a common topic, they usually contain some of the same information. It is the function of reduction and deletion transformations to get rid of some of the repeated information. For example, the sentence, "John doesn't like girls; therefore, John teases girls every time John gets a chance," is changed through a kind of noun phrase reduction transformation into, "John doesn't like girls; therefore, he teases them every time he gets a chance." and through deletion or "gapping" the sentences, "John likes ice cream. John likes cookies. And John likes chocolate syrup," become "John likes ice cream, cookies, and chocolate syrup." The deletion and reduction of elements within a discourse is evidence of the fact that juxtaposed sentences contain equivalent information. These types of transformations are used not only for succinctness, but also as transitional devices.

But while it is a requirement that two juxtaposed sentences must contain some common information, it is also a requirement that each sentence must provide some new information which has not been presented previously in the discourse. That is why the two following sentences cannot form a *normal* discourse: "This movie is free; it doesn't cost any money." The relationship between these two sentences is that one is a logical truth or tautology of the other. Tautologies are normally not accepted in the discourses of any language except possibly for emphasis or in order to give the listener a double shot at understanding the utterance. This is done in Persian where Arabic and Persian synonyms often occur together. In Early Modern English, Latin and English forms were also used this way. This is one reason that English has so many synonyms.

Whereas tautologies are excluded from normal discourse because they are totally redundant, contradictions are excluded from normal discourse because of an incompatibility. A tautology is logically true; that is if one part is true, the other part is necessarily also true. But contradictions are logically false; that is if one part is true, the other part is necessarily false. A discourse like, "John slept all day yesterday because he was so tired he couldn't get to sleep," is not possible because the two parts are incompatible. The shock effect of this kind of incompatibility is much of what nonsense is made of, for example:

> One bright day in the middle of the night,
> Two dead soldiers got up to fight,
> Back to back they faced each other,
> Pulled their swords, and shot each other....

We have established that two sentences in a discourse must have some relationship or shared topic with each other, they must be internally consistent, i.e., non contradictory, and there must be a purpose for the communication. Obviously, if the discourse has any effect, then the listener must have more information after the discourse than he did before. In other words, a discourse, and in fact each sentence within a discourse, must contain both old and new information. In the vocabulary of traditional grammarians this was identified as "topic and comment" or "theme and rheme." But in keeping with terminology used in recent literature on this topic, we will call the old information presuppositions and the new information assertions and inferences.

In an imperative sentence like, "Get the hell out of here!", there are a large number of presuppositions, many of which can be seen in the sentence itself, without considering additional linguistic or nonlinguistic context. It is presupposed, for example, that there is a person within hearing range of the speaker (or shouter), that this person understands English, that the speaker is firm in his opinion that the listener should leave, that he would rather risk offending the listener than have the listener stay, that the speaker has some control over the listener's actions, and that the speaker feels he can exert this control verbally. But in spite of the large numbers of presuppositions in this sentence, there is only one assertion, i.e., that the listener should leave the presence of the speaker.

There are certain types of presuppositions associated with commands, questions, and various kinds of other performatives. A sentence like, "John demolished the anthill," is intended only to convey information. The normal intonation for an English sentence like this is with the primary stress on the last word in the sentence, *anthill.* This is the new information in the sentence; it is the part being asserted. If we make the sentence passive, "The anthill was demolished by John," the stress is still on the last word of the sentence, but this time the last word is *John,* and this is therefore the asserted or new information. But whether the sentence is in its active, or in its passive form, it is possible to stress any word in the sentence, and the result is that whatever word is stressed represents the new or asserted information. In the sentence, *"John* demolished the anthill," we are asserting that it was John who did it; in "John *demolished* the anthill," we are asserting what he did to the anthill; in "John demolished *the* anthill," we are asserting that it was some special anthill that we both knew about; and in "John demolished the *anthill,"* we are asserting that it was an anthill that John demolished. In English, assertion is done through stress although in other languages the signaling may be something else. Any information which is presupposed is not asserted. Normally a sentence asserts one and only one thing. A sentence like, "The sky is grey," makes an assertion about the color of the sky; and the sentence, "The sky is dreary," makes an assertion about the relationship between the sky and the speaker, i.e., it makes him dreary. But when the first of these sentences is embedded into the second to form, "The grey sky is dreary," there is still only one assertion being made, and this assertion is the one marked by the predicate *is dreary.*

Although a sentence usually makes only one assertion, it often also makes many implications. Realizing that there must be a relationship or common topic between two sentences or between two parts of the same sentence, a listener could infer something about the meaning of the word *grey* if he knew only the word *dreary.* Or on the other hand, he could infer something about the word *dreary,* if he knew only the word *grey.* Such inferences as these are important not only in helping us to improve our vocabulary, but they also allow us as listeners to be able to project relationships onto the various parts of a discourse wherever these relationships are not overtly stated. As listeners, we must assume that the speaker is playing the language game with legitimate rules. Therefore if he says things in a discourse which are not obviously related to each other, we must assume that there is an unstated relationship, and it is our responsibility as listeners to provide the most reasonable connection possible in view of both the linguistic and nonlinguistic context, or else to point out to the speaker that we fail to see the connection, and force him to explicate that which he had previously implied.

In conclusion, it is not enough for us as linguists to develop machinery, no matter how detailed and rigorous, for analyzing or synthesizing the individual sentences of a particular language, because it is not the sentence, but rather the discourse which is the minimal unit of expression. Such concepts as *unique, anomalous, ambiguous,* and *vague* have no real meaning at the sentence level but are significant at the discourse level. If a sentence is ambiguous at the sentence level, but this ambiguity is resolved by the linguistic or nonlinguistic context, then the sentence is in fact nonambiguous. If a sentence is perfectly acceptable and grammatical as a sentence but contradicts something which has been said previously in the discourse, then it is anomalous. And the vagueness of a sentence depends not on its vagueness as an individual sentence, but rather its vagueness in its total linguistic and nonlinguistic context. Admittedly, it is not easy to deal with whole discourses and their relationships to the enormity of the real world, but this means only that we should work harder, not that we should throw up our hands in despair.

V. Semantic Features

The previous chapters pointed out some of the problems faced by linguists in trying to explain the semantic components of grammar. One of the problems faced by the generative semanticists working in terms of higher predicates is caused by the fact that breaking up a word and postulating its semantic components as higher predicates usually does not result in exact paraphrase, since, for example, a person can "cause someone to die" without literally "killing him." Many law suits revolve around this very question, with the courts trying to decide if the negligence which caused someone to die should be interpreted as a killing. Partially because of this difficulty in paraphrase, the generative semanticists defined their higher predicates as something different from regular lexical items. They suggest that "cause to die" as a paraphrase of "kill" should instead be "CAUSE to die," with "cause" differing from "CAUSE" in exactly the same way that "cause to die" differs from "kill." By separating their higher predicates from regular lexical items, they have set up a kind of semantic feature, even though they do not label it as such.

Semantic features are very important in case grammar. Even those grammarians who hold that the base component of a grammar consists of semantic cases rather than semantic features, define these cases in terms of such features as Animate vs. Inanimate, Actor vs. Receiver, etc. This means that they define Agent as the Animate Actor, Instrument as the Inanimate Cause, Experiencer as the Animate Receiver, Object as the Inanimate Receiver, etc. In determining deep cases, a majority of case grammarians rely on semantic features more than on syntactic matters. McCoy postulates as many as thirteen semantic features that are significant in distinguishing one case from another: Cause, Instigator, Performer, Intent, Effect, Source, Goal, Active, Control, Affected, Place, Transition, and Extent. Lambert has even more features than this, but she treats the word-specific distinguishers as well as the more general semantic markers. Any linguistic model that attempts to deal with the semantic component of language must account for the information conveyed by the various types of semantic features. This information might be handled in different ways in different models, but it must be handled. The purpose of this chapter is to investigate what it is that must be handled, i.e., what is the nature of semantic features.

In the past, linguists have generally listed the semantic features of a particular lexical item as determined by the discussion or the context in which the item appeared. Any features which were not germane to the discussion were largely ignored. Typically all semantic features were given the same status. Only a little work has been done in classifying semantic features along such lines as whether a feature has basically syntactic function such as marking agreement, whether it is a feature of the lexical item or of the sentence as a whole, and whether it is an objective real-world feature or a subjective perception feature or even a feature relating two lexical items in some way such as permission or obligation. We will look at these issues briefly, not in order to make a final, definitive statement, but rather to outline some of the questions that might be asked in setting up categories for semantic features. Merely as a rhetorical convenience, we will set up six tentative classes for semantic features. During the discussion the reader will undoubtedly see various ways in which this particular categorization can be improved, but it is hoped that having a sample classification system will be useful even if only to serve as a basis for criticism.

GRAMMATICAL FEATURES:

We will first consider grammatical features, by which we mean those semantic features which are overtly signaled in a language. Each of these grammatical features says something about the real world; however it should be cautioned that no grammatical features correlate perfectly with the real world. Here is a list of the grammatical features that are appropriate for English. Later each category will be discussed separately:

1. Person
   a. First
   b. Second
   c. Third
2. Number
   a. Singular
   b. Plural
   c. Other
3. Gender
   a. Masculine
   b. Feminine
   c. Neuter
   d. Common
4. Tense
   a. Past
   b. Present
   c. Future
5. Aspect
   a. Perfect
   b. Progressive
   c. Simple
   d. Overlapping
   e. Sequential
6. Voice
   a. Active
   b. Passive

7. Reference
   a. Definite
   b. Nondefinite
8. Mood
   a. Indicative
   b. Subjunctive
   c. Imperative
   d. Interrogative
   e. Conditional
9. Affirmation
   a. Affirmative
   b. Negative
10. Size
   a. Diminutive
   b. Large
   c. Comparative
   d. Other
11. Location
   a. Locative
   b. Movement
      (1) Accusative
      (2) Ablative
12. Time
   a. Temporal
   b. Sequence
13. Agent
14. Miscellaneous

It should first be pointed out that in English there is agreement between the subject and the predicate in person, number, tense, and mood. Thus, the -s ending on a verb is normally possible only under the condition that it is third person, singular, present tense, and indicative mood. The agreement in English between a pronoun and its antecedent is more complex. Personal and reflexive pronouns agree with their antecedents in person, number, and gender. Relative pronouns agree with their antecedents in none of these ways. However they are somewhat of a guide as to whether the antecedent is animate *(who, whom,* or *that)* or nonanimate *(which* or *that).*

The designation of person in English is primarily but not exclusively a function of the personal pronoun system. It refers to the communication act by specifying the speaker (first person), the person spoken to (second person), or the person spoken of (third person). The *-s* ending on a singular, present, indicative verb is a reinforcement of the personal pronoun system for the third person when singular referants are employed.

In English singular and plural expressions are distinguished reasonably well in the noun and pronoun systems and to a lesser extent in the verbal system. Here again, however, there is not a perfect match between linguistic plural and real-world plural as can be seen in such statements as "Everyone should take *his* seat," *"Man* does not live by bread alone," or *"Salmon* swim up that river to spawn." The italicized words in all these sentences refer to more than a single individual, but this is not signaled by any regular plural suffix. English also has overt signals for numbers more specific than simply plural or singular, but since these signals are all borrowed from other languages, the signaling is extremely haphazard and is bound to particular lexical items rather than being part of the grammar. Examples of such overt number affixes include the following:

One-half:	semi-, hemi-, demi-
One:	uni-, mono-
Two:	bi-, di-, tw-, du-
Three:	tri-
Four:	quadra-, tetra-, rect-, quart-
Five:	quint-, penta-
Six:	hex-, sex-
Seven:	sept-, hept-
Eight:	oct-
Nine:	nov-
Ten:	dec-

One hundred:	cent-
One thousand:	kilo-, mil-
One million:	mega-
More than one:	poli-, multi-

Such words as *group, herd, pride, pack, flock, gaggle, school,* and many others are also plural in concept. In addition to these overt number signals English has overt signals to indicate whether or not a noun is countable. If a noun is marked by such words as *many* or *a few,* it is countable and plural, but if it is marked by such expressions as *much* or *a little,* it is not countable; it is a mass noun. To make a mass noun countable we have to provide in the sentence some form of measurement which can be counted as in the following examples:

I want *some* ice cream. ⟶ I want *three* ice cream *cones.*
Give me *a little* sugar. ⟶ Give me *a few cubes* of sugar.
There's not *much* paint left. ⟶ There are not *many cans* of paint left.

Gender is also sometimes overtly marked in English, but here again, there is not a perfect correlation between the grammatical markings and the real-world situation. Gender in English is overtly signaled in the third person singular personal pronoun forms. Thus *he* is masculine, *she* is feminine, and *it* is neuter as when it refers to *the desk* or common as when it refers to *the baby.* The expression *one* as in "One shouldn't eat a heavy meal before swimming," also represents common as opposed to neuter gender. Neuter and common gender differ from each other in that something with neuter gender is neither male nor female but something with common gender is either male or female.

In the noun system there are a number of suffixes and prefixes which signal either the masculine or the feminine gender. A sample of masculine affixes includes *frat-* as in *fraternity, patr-* as in *patron, fellow* as in *fellow worker, lord* as in *landlord, boy* as in *cowboy,* and *guy* as in *fall guy.* A sample of feminine affixes includes *-ess* as in *hostess, -ette* as in *usherette, -ix* as in *aviatrix, maid* as in *chambermaid, wife* as in *fishwife, soror-* as in *sorority,* and *mater-* as in *maternal.* With animal names there is often a contrast between the feminine and masculine forms as in *cow-bull, doe-stag, nanny goat-billy goat, ewe-ram,* and *hen-rooster.*

But with gender, as with person and number, the fit between the language and the real world is by no means perfect. Many languages have grammatical gender rather than natural gender. In these languages there are a great many arbitrary gender assignments. In French, for example, *la bicyclette* is feminine while *le train* is masculine. Since grammatical gender does not relate to the semantic aspect of language, it is not surprising that a particular real-world item such as *nose* or *river* or *chair* might be masculine in one language, feminine in another, and neuter in a third. Although English has natural gender rather than grammatical gender, there is still not a perfect fit between linguistic gender and sex. We might refer to a ship as *she;* when we go for gas at a service station we might use the expression, "Fill *'er* up," and even when there are women as well as men in a room we might ask everyone to hold up *his* right hand. And when we use such words as pen*man*ship, *master*piece, *fellow*ship, *man*kind, anchor*man,* and *brother*hood we don't mean to exclude females. But many contemporary writers feel that at least on a subconscious level words like these serve as keep-out signs to women. In studying the English language from a feminist viewpoint they have made some interesting observations about particular usages which reflect the values society has placed on males and females respectively. For one thing they have found that masculine and feminine counterparts communicate much more than gender. For example in the following list, the masculine words have positive connotations while the corresponding feminine terms have either negative, trivial, or sexual connotations.

FEMALE EXPRESSION:	MALE EXPRESSION:
aviatrix	aviator
governess	governor
madam	sir
majorette	major
mistress	master
poetess	poet
priestess	priest
spinster	bachelor
squaw	brave
stewardess	steward
witch	wizard
woman on the street	man on the street

Tense is another grammatical feature. It is signaled overtly in English verbs by such suffixes as *-s,* and *-ed,* and covertly in certain

English nouns such as: *last night, Tuesday,* and *tomorrow;* prepositional phrases such as *in a year,* and *over the summer;* and clauses such as *when school is out* and *the day that you came.* It is necessary to make a distinction between the grammatical concept of tense, which is linked to certain affixes, and time, which is linked to the real world.

In the same way it is necessary to make a distinction between grammatical aspect and real-world aspect. Such concepts as sequential and overlapping may be thought of as a kind of aspect; however, they are shown only through lexical items rather than through grammatical signals. Aside from these lexical kinds of gender and the unmarked neutral aspect, there are two grammatical aspects in English: perfect and progressive. An English perfect expression contains some form of the verb *have* followed by a past participle as in "He has eaten." An English progressive expression contains some form of the verb *be* followed by a present participle as in "He is eating." But here again there is by no means a perfect match between the linguistic, grammatical aspect and the real-world aspect. For example, there are some verbs which cannot be made grammatically progressive. Notice for example that when sentences like, "I know that he is here," or "I think that he is smart," are made progressive the resulting sentences, *"I am knowing that he is here," and *"I am thinking that he is smart," are ungrammatical unless they are spoken in an unusual situation such as a game. One reason for this is that such verbs as *know* and *think* are inherently durative and the grammatical progressive expansion of adding *be* and *-ing* is therefore incompatible. The non-expansion of a verb in English usually signals a fairly long-term truth, and these truths are in nature durative. When a person makes an unqualified statement, i.e., a statement without verbal expansion or adverbial modification, like, "I play basketball," or "I study hard," or "I hate examinations," he is making a statement not specifically about the present time, but rather about a general truth, and general truths of this nature are not instantaneous but durative. On the other hand if he says, "I am playing basketball," or "I am studying hard," (notice he cannot say, *"I am hating examinations"), he is limiting the duration rather than broadening it.

Just as English progressive expressions are semantically quite similar in meaning to some simple nonprogressive expressions, English present perfect constructions are semantically quite similar to simple past constructions. A present perfect construction communicates that the action has been completed or "perfected" at the present time of the speaking or writing. The statement, "I ate," and the statement, "I have eaten," have similar time reference, but for different reasons. In the present perfect construction "I have eaten," the action is completed (or perfected) before the present time; in the past construction "I ate," the action happened in the past. To the extent that "completed before present" is similar to "past," then, these two sentences have the same time reference.

Voice is another type of grammatical feature. The active voice is the normal, expected situation, in which the actor of a sentence functions as the subject of the sentence, and the thing acted upon functions as the direct object. A passive transformation shifts the receiver of the action into the subject position and shifts the actor into a post-verbal position marked with the preposition *by*. When in the surface structure the actor is part of a prepositional phrase it becomes deletable. The passive transformation in English can make either direct objects or indirect objects into subjects in the following way:

ORIGINAL SENTENCE: John gave the apples to Mary.
DIRECT OBJECT BECOMING SUBJECT: The apples were given (to) Mary (by John).
INDIRECT OBJECT BECOMING SUBJECT: Mary was given the apples (by John).

The basic effect of the passive transformation is a change in focus. Typically the new information comes at the end of the sentence in English. Therefore, the active sentence "John's best friend murdered John," if spoken without contrastive stress, would be uttered in two situations: (1) when the information to be communicated, that is the new or surprise information, is the entire act, or (2) when the information to be communicated is the last word of the sentence: John. In both cases, the new information comes at the end: the only difference is that in the first instance it extends further toward the front. In a sentence which has been made passive, it is again usually the end information which is new. Usually, the sentence, "John was murdered by his best friend," would be made to stress the fact that it was the best friend who was the villain. When the agent phrase, "by his best friend," is deleted to yield, "John was murdered," the resulting sentence, again assuming no contrastive stress in speech, is focusing on the act of murder rather than on the actor (John's best friend) or on the receiver (John). One purpose of the passive transformation, therefore is to change focus, or in other words, to change the distribution of old and new information in a sentence.

The passive transformation differs from one language to another. In English, the passive transformation does four things: (1) it takes the actor to the end of the sentence; (2) it takes the receiver to the beginning of the sentence; (3) it expands the verb phrase, *be + -en;* and (4) it marks the actor with the preposition *by*. It is interesting that most Indo-European languages have passive transformations consisting of these four components, except that the lexical items introduced are different. But even more interesting is that all languages have ways of changing the distribution of old and new information. In some cases, this is done by passive or reflexive transformations which affect the focus by changing elements around with respect to each other, by deleting certain elements to "expose" something to be focused on, or by adding a focus morpheme such as *ka* in Japanese. In other cases, this is done not at the syntactic, but at the lexical level. This can be illustrated with an example from English where *farmer* is an active noun, while *planter* when referring to the brick construction in the front of a home which contains plants, is a passive noun. Since it is not an actor, but is rather a receiver of the action, it is not given the same semantic value as is *farmer*. Or consider various converse relationships. In order to passivize the expression, "John gave me Mary's notes," it is possible to use either the syntactic passive, "I was given Mary's notes by John," or the lexical passive, "I received Mary's notes from John." Thus, such converse pairs as *give-receive, buy-sell, amuse-annoy, imply-infer,* etc. have the effect of expressing this active-passive relationship in which the distribution of old and new information is changed. Such converse relationships are probably present in all human languages.

Reference is another grammatical feature which is usually but not always overtly signaled in English. Quantifiers such as *all* or *no* give an exact notion of the relationship between the lexical expression and whatever this expression refers to in the real world. *All* is used when reference is to a class of items such as in, "all the dogs," "all kinds of people," or "all my money." Even the expression *all day* can be analyzed as a shortened form of something like "all the minutes (or hours) of the day." Because we expect *all* to relate perfectly to the real world, writers, debators, and logicians are cautioned about being extra careful whenever they make a statement containing *all.* In a similar way, *no* is used in reference to a class, but this time the class has zero members as in "No children came," and, "There have been no accidents." Again we expect a perfect correlation between the linguistic expression and the real world. Such quantifiers as *most* and *many* show a partial correlation between the linguistic expression and the real world.

All languages have the capability of showing a perfect positive correlation, a perfect negative correlation, and a range of additional positive and negative correlations between the linguistic expression and the real world. Languages can indicate the reference of not only classes of things, but of individual things as well. In English, the word *the* (or *this, that, these,* and *those)* in conjunction with either a prior reference or a later restrictive modifier indicates a unique relationship between the linguistic form and a particular item in the real world. Both in the sentence, "A man entered the bank; the man was carrying a gun," and in the sentence, "The man who entered the bank was carrying a gun," the expression *man* is referring to one and only one real-world item.

Capitalization is another technique in English surface structure to show a unique relationship between the linguistic expression and the real-world item, whether this capitalization is used for a person, as in *John Jones, the President,* and *He* (referring to God), or for a place, as in *Chicago* and *the West.* However some English time expressions are capitalized even though they do not completely limit the linguistic expression to a particular real-world item, for example *Monday* or *December* (compare the uncapitalized *yesterday, today, tomorrow,* etc.). Nevertheless, capitalization is a very common technique for showing unique reference, and this might possibly help account for the fact that the first person singular personal pronoun, *I,* is the only one capitalized in English. Because they can refer to more than one person, such pronouns as *you, they,* and *we* are more ambiguous as to their exact reference than is *I.* However on the basis of this kind of reasoning, *he, she,* and *it* should also be capitalized, since these pronouns can be used if and only if there is a clearly determined noun phrase in the immediate environment. Perhaps *I* is capitalized simply as a mark of the egocentric relationship which exists between a writer and that particular pronoun.

A fascinating fact about language, or rather, about our ability to conceptualize and symbolize the real world, is that it is possible to make specific and definite reference to things which do not exist. Almost all English speakers will understand, and will know what is being referred to when a statement is made like, "the unicorn in my pasture eats nothing but grass." In real life the speaker has neither a unicorn nor a pasture; nevertheless listeners probably get a clear mental picture of both a unicorn and a pasture. But still *a unicorn* is less of a referring expression than is *a pasture,* probably because pastures exist in our experiences while unicorns do not. But at some other time and some other place (in a science fiction novel, for example), the situation might be reversed with unicorns being real and pastures imagined.

There are overt devices for signaling whether reference is to real-world or imaginary-world items. To some extent in English, and to a much greater extent in some other languages, a statement in the indicative mood has a real-world correspondence; whereas a statement in the subjunctive mood corresponds only to possible- (not real-) world phonomena. It is a hypothetical situation. The conditional mood marks a relationship between the real world and something that might occur. This connection is shown through such expressions in English as *if* and *unless,* as in, "If he studies hard he will get a good grade," and "Unless he studies hard, he won't get a good grade." Causative expressions like *nevertheless, because, therefore,* and *although* sometimes communicate this same relationship, as in, "He won't study hard; nevertheless he'll get a good grade," "He'll get a good grade because he studies hard," "He's been studying; therefore he'll get a good grade," and "Although he won't study, he'll get a good grade." Although the syntax of these various expressions is heterogeneous, they, along with many other such expressions, seem to have the same semantic function of demonstrating a possible happening's dependency on another possible happening.

While the English indicative mood contrasts with the subjunctive and conditional moods in determining real versus imaginary worlds, the indicative mood contrasts with the imperative and the interrogative moods in determining the function of the particular speech act. The indicative mood is used for describing or explaining something which the hearer was not formerly aware of. The imperative is used to elicit an action and the interrogative to elicit a verbal response. There are often formal signals to indicate mood. In English the conditional mood is signaled by special forms of the verb *to be* as in, "If I were planning to go I would have ordered tickets," or the past tense form of other verbs as in, "Even if I did want a babysitter, I wouldn't ask *her.*" Past tense forms of this type do not refer to past time.

Except in such communications as, "Joan, you take the books; Sam, you bring the tests; and Kelvin, you bring the tape recorder," English imperatives do not have expressed subjects. And the verb is usually in its noninflected form, for example, "Be good!", "Come back soon," and "Turn right at the next corner."

English yes-no interrogatives typically show an inversion of the subject and either the auxiliary or the main verb as in:

He is here.	Is he here?
She can come.	Can she come?
They danced fast.	Did they dance fast?

If there is no verb which can be inverted (either a form of *be* or a modal) then some form of *do* is added to the sentence.

But a person cannot always rely on the linguistic signals of the surface structure to determine the mood of an expression. The questions, "Isn't it a little warm in here?" and "Is there any butter on the table?" might really be uttered as polite requests to have someone open a window or pass the butter respectively. The expectations of the speaker are such that he has made a request or command rather than asked a question. And when a teacher says to a student, "We'll do better on the next test, won't we?" she's requesting a change in behavior rather than a yes-no answer. And if a person asks, "How are things going?" he usually doesn't want a specific answer, even if one were possible, but instead wants to set up lines of communication between himself and the speaker. And if a person says "Damn it!" or "Go to Hell!" or "I'll be damned!" he doesn't mean any of these things literally. In fact, it is often possible for different moods to refer to exactly the same situation. For example in offering someone candy, it can be done with a question as in, "Would you like a piece of candy?", a command as in, "Have a piece of candy," an indicative statement as in, "Here's some candy," or a conditional statement as in, "If you'll try some of this candy, I think you'll like it."

Usually the subjunctive in English is overtly signaled by the modal *could* as in, "Well, it could be true, but I doubt it!" However other modals such as *would, may,* and *might* can also be said to indicate an unreal situation. Subjunctive marking in English is closely associated with conditional constructions. However, the non-reality of a speech act is usually not signaled grammatically in English, so users of the language must rely on more subtle lexical clues to communicate this information. The main device used is that of postulating impossible (or highly improbable) events. A story which tells about a baby being born from his mother's ear, or about a lumberjack forming the Grand Canyon by dragging large trees behind him, or a man so huge that a normal-sized person could hide in his snuff box, or a bunch of ducks which (or should we say *who?*) can talk to each other in English must necessarily have reference to some imaginary world, as must a story which tells about trips to other galaxies and superhuman robots, etc. It is because we know most of the possibilities and limitations of the real world that we can decide at least tentatively whether a writer or speaker is referring to a real or made-up world. Storytellers have developed set phrases which communicate to the listener that an unreal world is being described, for example, "Once upon a time . . . . ," "In the never-never land of . . . . ," or the Persian "Once it was, once it wasn't . . . ." Any discourse which can be described as fantasy, dream, wish, hope, etc. has the feature of unreal. Fantasy, as opposed to nonfiction and realistic fiction, has the feature unreal throughout the entire discourse. Even in nonfiction, this feature of unreal can be operative for short stretches of what is called figurative or metaphorical language. In our culture there are many worlds which we talk about even though they are unreal, for example, mythology, TV soap operas, movies, cartoons, books, etc. In talking about such worlds it is not uncommon to refer to things which have no extensional meaning. These words might lack a referent because they don't exist, e.g., *dragon, unicorn, genie, Santa Claus, the good fairy, the Easter bunny,* etc.; because they are extinct, e.g., *dinosaur, trilobite, brachiopod, pterodactyl,* etc.; or because they exist only in imaginative literature, e.g., *Brer Rabbit, Yogi Bear, the Mad Hatter*, etc.

Another grammatical feature to consider is negative and its opposite, affirmative. In English the negative element can be attached to a count noun as with *nobody,* a mass noun as with *inability,* an adjective as with *illegible,* an adverb as with *infrequently,* or a verb as with *untie.* In addition, it can negate the entire sentence rather than a single word as in, "Such a creature doesn't exist." or it can negate a clause it is not really a part of as in, "I didn't want to go." Here the negation applies to the going rather than the wanting. A different way to write this sentence would be, "I wanted not to go." As with other grammatical features, negation is sometimes an inherent feature of the lexical item rather than being overtly signaled as a prefix. Again, this negative inherent feature can be part of a count noun. For example, a *laggard* is someone who is not ambitious. An example of negation in a mass noun is the word *awkwardness* which indicates a lack of gracefulness. The adjective *poor* means not rich, the adverb *seldom* means not often, and the verb *prevent* means not to allow something. More will be said about the contrast of affirmative and negative elements in a later discussion of antonyms.

Another semantic feature which is often overtly signaled is size. Suffixes frequently used for this purpose are *-ette* as in *novelette,* *-ling* as in *duckling, -let* as in *piglet, mini-* as in *miniature,* and *micro-* as in *microcosm.* There seems to be a very high correlation between the semantic feature diminutive and the semantic feature feminine. It is often the case that a suffix meaning feminine at the same time means small. However an exception to this rule is the modifier *queen size* as in *queen size panty hose* which is used as a euphemism for an extra large size of women's clothing, but when this refers to something used by both men and women, such as beds, *queen size* is one size smaller than *king size.*

Such prefixes as *super-, extra-, over-,* and *out-,* are used to indicate a great quantity or quality. Such prefixes as *infer-* and *under-* are used to indicate a small quantity or quality. As with other grammatical suffixes, size is often determinable from the bare lexical item without any affix at all. The following animal terms for example have the semantic feature of young, and in relation to this, smallness: *baby, bunny, calf, chick, child, colt, cub, fawn, foal, kid, kitten, lamb, pony,* and *pup(py).*

In considering the semantic breakdown of the concept of size, it is not feasible to have only a binary feature representation such as plus or minus diminutive, or plus or minus large. In order to represent the real world accurately, size must be considered a continuum ranging from very large to very small with many points in between. Consider the lexical concept of "place to live," for example. Mostly on the basis of size, this concept might be represented by the following English items: *castle, palace, mansion, house, cottage, apartment, cabin, shack, shanty, studio,* and *efficiency.* Or consider the example of "a very hard piece of earth." When a person sees one of these items he can refer to it as a *monolith,* a *boulder,* a *stone,* a *rock,* or a *pebble* depending on its size. If he sees many of these things and they are of a fairly uniform size, he may refer to the entire mass as *gravel, sand, dirt, clay,* or *silt.* Again the term would be chosen depending on the size of the particles in question. Units of measure such as *gallon, quart, pint, cup, tablespoon, teaspoon,* and *pinch,* or *millenium, century, decade, year, month, day, hour, minute,* and *second* are also distinguishable from each other by size. Size distinctions are extremely common in any language, but since there is usually a continuum of size in the speaker's mind, it would be difficult for this kind of relative relationship to be overtly marked in the surface structure of a language. However, we have been told that Bantu languages do this.

Another grammatical feature is comparison. When this is overtly marked, the marking is done with the suffix *-er,* (with *-est* for the superlative), or the particle *more,* (with *most* for the superlative). Negative comparatives are marked by *less* (with *least* for the superlative). These comparative markers can be attached either to adjectives as in *taller,* or to adverbs of manner as in *more rapidly.* But here again, there is not a perfect correlation between the semantic feature and the surface structure indication of this feature, because nearly always when an adjective or adverb is used a comparison is intended. When a person says, "An elephant is big," he means "An elephant is bigger than the average animal." When a person says "Dumbo is small," he means "Dumbo is smaller than most elephants." The implied comparison of sentences containing adjectives or adverbs is of the modified noun or verb as compared with the average in the class to which it belongs. When a speaker says, "That red ant moves rapidly," he is comparing the red ant to other ants which is the class of objects containing that particular ant. But if he says, "Ants move rapidly," he is comparing ants to other insects which is the class containing ants.

Locative and temporal expressions are overtly marked, also. There are many subclasses of locative expressions and many affixes for marking location. For example there is *-dom* as in *kingdom* and *loc-* as in *locality*. For indicating the position in front of something there is *fore-* as in *forehead*. For indicating a position within something there is *intra-* as in *intramuscular* and *intro-* as in *introduction*. For indicating a distance from something there is *tele-* as in *teletype* and *peri-* as in *periscope*. There is also *out-* as in *outdoors, over-* as in *overcoat, super-* as in *superscript,* and *supra-* as in *supranasal.* For indicating a position below there is *sub-* as in *submarine* and *under-* as in *underclothing.* There are also a number of affixes which indicate a change of location. Regular movement is signaled by *-mobile-* as in *mobility* or *automobile.* Movement toward something is signaled by *ad-* as in *admit, -in* as in *inhale, pro-* as in *progress,* and *-ward(s)* as in *earthward.* Movement away from something is signaled by *ab-* as in *abscond, apo-* as in *apogee, dis-* as in *discard, ex-* as in *exile,* and *off-* as in *offspring.* Other expressions of motion include the concept of going around something which is signaled by *by-* as in *bypass* and *circum-* as in *circumvent.* The concept of going across is signaled by *trans-* as in *transatlantic,* and the concept of going from one place to another is signaled by *inter-* as in *interstate.*

There is also signaling of temporal concepts. The general concept of time is often signaled by *chron-* as in *synchronize.* Specific units of time can be signaled by such affixes as *men-* meaning month in *menstrual, annu-* meaning year in *anniversary,* and *cent-* meaning one hundred in *century.* If something is earlier in time this can be signaled by *ante-* as in *antecedent* or *pre-* as in *preface.* If something is later in time this can be signaled by *post-* as in *postmortem.* The very first in time or at least very early in time is signaled by *proto-* as in *protozoan.* Something that lasts over a long period of time can have the suffix *-dur* as in *endure.* The suffix *-iary* indicates a sequence as in *tertiary* and the prefix *re-* indicates a repetition or reversal as in *remarry* or *return.*

Even though there may be a large number of affixes in English which signal spatial or temporal concepts there are also a great many lexical items which contain spatial or temporal concepts as part of their meaning, such as *Chicago* and *home* for locatives and *tomorrow* and *1924* for temporals. These have no overt signal except the shape of the lexical item itself to indicate that a spatial or temporal concept is present.

The concept of actor or agent is also overtly signaled at the lexical level for some words in English. The most obvious of the agentive suffixes are *-ant* as in *applicant*, *-er* as in *composer*, and *-ist* as in *terrorist*. Such suffixes as *-an* in *musician*, *-smith* as in *locksmith*, and *-man* as in *hangman* communicate that someone is a doer of the action given in the word stem. The receiver of an action is sometimes marked by *-ee* which contrasts with the actor as can be seen in the pair of words *employer-employee*. These suffixes are a sufficient but not necessary condition for the existence of the semantic feature. *Pilot, secretary,* and *drunkard* are just as active as *aviator, typist,* and *drinker* even though the former words do not have formal agent suffixes.

The final grammatical feature which we will consider is cause. The three verbal markers which most frequently indicate cause are *-en-* as in *encourage* or *darken, -ify* as in *beautify,* and *-ize* as in *centralize.* As can be seen from the last examples, the feature "cause" usually entails the feature "inchoative" which means "to become." *Beautify* means to "*cause* to *become* beautiful." Here again, as in all of the other cases, it is not necessary for something to be marked with a causative ending in order for there to be a causative element of meaning present. In the sentence, "John broke the window," *break* is just as much a causative verb as is *shorten* in, "John shortened the rope."

There are a great many other affixes in English which carry a particular semantic meaning. Most of these affixes are taken either from Latin or Greek. As a demonstration of the nature and the range of such affixes, a number are listed below:

PREFIX:	MEANING:	EXAMPLE:
aqua-	water	aquamarine
ambi-	going around	ambivalent
ana-	parts	analysis

PREFIX:	MEANING:	EXAMPLE:
auto-	self	automobile
bene-	well	benefit
biblio-	book	bibliography
bio-	life	biography
celest-	heaven	celestial
cephal-	head	cephalic
co-	with	co-pilot
cord-	heart	cordial
cosmos-	universe	cosmonaut
crypt-	code	cryptic
dent-	tooth	dentures
dict-	talk	dictaphone
digni-	worthy	dignitary
don-	give	donate
form-	shape	formation
frag-	break	fragment
frater-	brother	fraternal
geo-	earth	geography
hetero-	different	heterosexual
homo-	same	homogenized
hydro-	water	hydrophobia
infra-	beneath	infrared
iso-	equal	isogloss
liber-	free	liberty
lith-	stone	lithograph
lum-	light	luminary
manu-	hand	manufacture
mater-	mother	maternity
ment-	mind	mental
naut-/nav-	sailor	nautical
nucl-	nut or center	nuclear
omni-	all	omnipotent
ovu-	egg	ovulation
para-	at the side of	paraphrase
pater-	father	paternal
per-	through	pervasive
phys-	body	physician
psych-	mind	psychologist
sanct-	holy	sanctimonious
soror-	sister	sorority
spect-	see	spectator
sphere-	round	spheroid

PREFIX:	MEANING:	EXAMPLE:
stabil-	stationary	stabilize
stella-	star	stellar
sym-	form or symbol	symmetrical
syn-	with, together	syndicate
terre-	earth	terrestrial
therm-	heat	thermometer
uni-	one	unicycle
verb-	word	verbose
vis-	see	visionary

SUFFIX OR INFIX:	MEANING:	EXAMPLE:
-able-	ability	disagreeable
-acy	government	democracy
-carn-	flesh or meat	reincarnation
-cide	kill	insecticide
-cycle	round	bicycle
-derm	skin	epiderm
-dext-	hand	ambidextrous
-dict	speech	verdict
-form	shape	conform
-graph	picture	photograph
-hab-	live	inhabitant
-mani	craving	pyromania
-meter	measuremt	speedometer
-ness	quality of	greatness
-nym	name or meaning	synonym
-pathos-	suffering	sympathetic
-ped-pod-	foot	orthopodist
-phobia	fear, hatred	hydrophobia
-phone	sound	megaphone
-scope	see	kaleidoscope
-scribe-	write	inscription
-theo-	God	atheist
-therapy	heal	psychotherapy
-zoo-	animal	protozoan

In concluding this section three important points should be made. First, every form which has an overt signal of some kind has a corresponding form without the signal (at least in the deep structure), and it is the unmarked form which is more basic and the marked form which is derived from the unmarked form by the addition of a suffix. Second, any treatment which has a semantic bias must consider all forms containing a semantic feature to be equivalent in this respect regardless of whether or not the semantic feature happens to be manifested in the surface structure. And third, there is no reason to believe that all semantic features will be signaled by such things as affixes, function words, or special word order in the surface structure of any particular language, or indeed in a composite of all languages. The semantic features are universal and apply to all languages equally; the surface structure manifestations in a particular language can give a linguist insights into the semantic component, however, it should be cautioned that although there is a relationship between the surface structure and the deep structure (semantics), this relationship is far from perfect, and whenever there is a conflict between the two, it is the native speaker's intuition about the semantic component which should take priority over the surface markings in resolving the conflict.

INHERENT FEATURES:

Grammatical features are those features which happen to be marked in the surface structure of a particular language. Inherent features are those features which have real-world significance. Therefore, to a very large extent, a grammatical feature is a special kind of inherent feature—one which is explicitly marked in the surface structure of some languages. This means that in a gross way, all the grammatical features which have so far been discussed are actually marked inherent features. There are some differences, however, as can be seen in the contrasting terminology which grammarians have used. Such terms as *tense, grammatical gender, progressive,* and *marked plural* are terms used to describe grammatical features. The inherent features which contrast with these four concepts would be *time, natural gender, durative,* and *plural.* To this point, we have been discussing features which are sometimes marked in the surface structure of a particular language—English. There are a great many semantic features which are never marked in this way, but each particular lexical item of any language has a number of these semantic features. If you asked a large number of native speakers whether or not the word contained a particular feature, there would be a great deal of consistency in their answers. If they gave inconsistent answers for a particular word, this would indicate that the word was ambiguous or vague in reference to this particular feature.

Let us assume that there are three basic functions of words in a sentence: naming, predicating, and modifying. There will be a later discussion of predicate and adverbial features. But right now let us consider the inherent features related to "naming words", i.e., nouns. Semantic features accompanying nouns have been the most thoroughly discussed in the literature as *inherent features,* and it has been shown that there is a hierarchical ordering for such features. The lexical item *Nicolette,* for example, is [+Human], and this means that it is also automatically [+Animate], [+Count], [+Concrete], etc. These lower level features that need not be specified because they are the automatic result of higher level features are called *redundancy features.* It might be argued that *Nicolette* is a shorthand not only for the four features mentioned above, and for [+Definite], and [−Male], which are additional concepts labeled by various linguists as inherent features, but also for [+Mammal], [+Potent], [+Linguistic], [+Complex Thought], [+Biped], [+Vertebrate], etc., as well. In fact, there is an almost unlimited number of features which distinguish a particular person from all other things. And the name *Nicolette* is a shorthand for all these features; however, we must not feel obligated to indicate in a linguistic description all the conceptual apparatus inherent in a word. Such a task would be futile. It is possible only to indicate the higher level features; most of the lower level features will be an automatic result of the higher level features and therefore not stated in a linguistic description.

In the first part of this chapter, we made frequent mention of the fact that the fit between the semantic reality and the linguistic representation of this semantic reality is certainly not always a tight fit. The same problem arises with the inherent features used with the naming words presently under discussion. First, in the real world it would seem that some things are of such a nature that they can be counted while other substances cannot. Yet the expressions *camping gear* and *items for use in camping* both refer to exactly the same thing in the real world, although the first is a non-count expression while the second is a count expression. Another example is the

English non-count expression *furniture* which is translated into many languages as a count expression.

Or consider the feature *proper*. The assumption is sometimes made that there is a perfect correlation between the concept *proper* and the concept *definite*, but in fact the former is a term appopriate to the surface structure, which often reflects deep structure facts, while the latter has nothing to do with surface structure; it is totally a deep structure term. As an example, contrast the sentence, "They named their son Brunhilda," which contains a proper noun, with the sentence, "They named their son something outlandish," which does not contain a proper noun. Both of these sentences could very well be referring to the same real-world fact, and both the expression *Brunhilda* and the expression *something outlandish* are definite. But of the two, only *Brunhilda* is a proper noun. It is not possible to trust a certain word out of context to have particular inherent features. *Tuesday* may be plus or minus human; *Kelly* may be plus or minus masculine; *Red* may be the name of a person or a dog, etc. It might also be desirable to break down some of these features. Linguistic evidence might be given, for example, to support breaking down the feature *concrete* into features *solid, liquid,* and *gas.* If this were done, *solid* would end up as plus or minus count, for example *iron* would be [−count] and *trees* would be [+count]. But *liquid* and *gas* would both end up as [−count]. Empirical (i.e., testable) evidence will be required in order to make this type of decision. Another example of a problem to be resolved by empirical evidence is whether or not such words as *mutton, venison, veal, beef* and *pork* (or *sausage, bacon,* or *ham*) contain the inherent features *sheep, deer, young cow, cow,* and *pig* respectively. An a final example is whether or not the words *close, here, this, these, me, come, bring, neighbor, friend, near, in, import, entrance,* and *home* share a semantic feature with each other that is not present in *far, there, that, those, he, go, take, foreigner, enemy, away, out, export, exit,* and *abroad.*

PREDICATE FEATURES:

To this point we have discussed two types of inherent features. The first features we talked about were the grammatical features, so called because these particular inherent features become manifested in the surface structure. The second set were called inherent features because this is the term that has been used most extensively in the literature to refer to this kind of covert inherent feature. There are three types of semantic features remaining to be discussed—predicate features, adverbial features, and perception features. It might be argued that these last three types of semantic features are inherent features just as the first two types are. We do not intend to answer that question, except to point out that the term *inherent feature* seems to imply that the feature resides in the particular lexical item, and it is not precisely true that these last three types of features totally reside in the lexical items. Predicate features are relational, and they therefore reside in all the lexical items being related. Adverbial features frequently have the entire statement as their domain, and so it is not really proper to say that they reside in a particular lexical item and in the minds of the communicators. One person will ascribe very different perception features to a particular lexical item than will another person.

But returning to predicate features, they can be listed as *cause, instigator, performer, intent, effect, source, goal, active, control, affected, inchoative,* etc. The reason that they are termed predicate features is that whenever such features are present, they can be extracted from a lower sentence and placed as the predicate of a higher sentence through the process of predicate lifting. For example, in the sentence, "John ran the mile in four minutes," in reference to the rest of the sentence, the expression *John,* contains the predicate features *instigation, intention, performance,* etc., and these can be extracted out and placed as higher predicates, as in "John instigated...," "John intended...," "John performed...," etc. It should be noted that these predicate features, like the inherent features discussed earlier are often hierarchically related, so that when *instigation* is present, it is perfectly predictable that *intention* and *performance* will also be present. It should also be pointed out that these predicate features often occur in pairs, like *cause-effect, actor-receiver, controller-controlled, source-goal,* etc., and that the first of these pairs of features is usually related to the subject in English and many other languages, while the second member of the pair is usually related to the direct object or some other oblique case. This subject will be more fully treated in Chapter VI, "Semantic Cases or Logical Arguments."

Because predicate features are relational, they are not totally relevant for one-place predicates, e.g., states. For example, in the sentence, "Ice is a solid," none of the features mentioned have relevance because all of these predicate features indicate an action of some kind. There is one feature, however, which relates states to other states, the *inchoative.* Such verbs as *evaporate, liquify, melt,* and *freeze* contain the feature inchoative and can therefore be paraphrased with the lexical item *become,* as follows: *become gas, become liquid,* and *become solid,* respectively. But notice that both *melt* and *condense* have the same paraphrase *become liquid,* even though they are not synonyms. A more correct paraphrase for *melt* would be *change from solid to liquid,* while *condense* would probably mean *change from gas to liquid;* therefore the source(*solid* or *gas*) is required as well as the goal (*liquid*) in order to distinguish these two words.

ADVERBIAL FEATURES:

There is a long tradition among grammarians to consider expressions like *in the classroom,* and *yesterday* as adverbs, implying that such expressions modify the verb of a sentence. But consider a sentence like, "John gave Mary a kiss in the classroom yesterday." In this sentence, *in the classroom* and *yesterday* have a close affinity to the verb *gave,* but in fact they modify the entire proposition "John gave Mary a kiss," rather than merely the verb *gave.* Now consider a slightly larger discourse:

John gave Mary a kiss in the classroom yesterday. Mary was displeased so she hit him with a book and bloodied his nose.

In this micro-discourse, *in the classroom* and *yesterday* can be said to modify the second sentence as much as they modify the first. There are at least five different kinds of adverbial features which behave in this way: place, time, manner, extent, and reason. To explain these adverbial features, let us view a sentence as a miniature play. In a play there are often a hero, a villain, and some props. In like manner, a sentence often contains an Agent (animate actor), an Experiencer (animate receiver of the action), an Instrument (inanimate cause), an Object (inanimate thing manipulated), etc. Whether such case concepts as Agent, Experiencer, Instrument, Object, etc. are relevant only at the sentence level, or whethey they also have some relevance at the discourse level, is presently open to question. But back to our metaphor. The adverbial features which are presently being discussed are parallel to the setting of a play, and in fact, such concepts as place, time, reason, extent, and manner have the same relevance in a play (or more appropriately a scene within a play) as they have in a discourse. In a discourse, as in a play, once the place is established, it is assumed that this place does not change unless there is some overt statement that it is changing. The same is true with time, reason, etc., except that each language has particular peculiarities as to which of these adverbial features must be redundantly signaled because of the nature of the language. In English, for example, it is necessary that all finite verbs show tense (past or non-past), even when the tense has already been firmly established previously in the discourse. In Hopi or Thai, on the other hand, there is no such requirement; in these languages, and many others, the signaling of tense is optional (in the adverbial system) rather than obligatory.

The meaning of reason, extent, and manner is less obvious than is that of place and time. In a play, reason would be termed motivation. In a sentence, or in a play, it is the reason which explains why a particular thing is done, and this can usually be expressed in a cause-effect relationship. In a play, extent would refer to the amount of action that is put into a character. Such terms as *underacting* or *overacting* are used by directors to indicate an inappropriate amount of action. In a play, manner would refer to the quality of action. We are making a contrast between quality, which we call manner, and quantity, which we call extent. On the linguistic level, reason would be signaled by *because, therefore, thus, although, nevertheless, still,* etc. Extent would be signaled by *greatly, twenty-five gallons, rapidly,* etc. And manner would be signaled by *like a clumsy oaf, well, better than his sister,* etc.

It is not a requirement, however, that these adverbial features have their own autonomy of expression in a sentence or discourse. The distinction between *walk* on the one hand and on the other hand such words as *amble, clomp, dash, gallop, goosestep, hike, jog, limp, lope, march, meander, plod, prance, promenade, ramble, romp, rove, scamper, sprint, stagger, stalk, stomp, stray, stride, stroll, strut, traipse, tramp, trot,* and *wander* is basically a result of the verbal incorporation of reason, extent, and manner. It is obvious from the above list of verbs that these three adverbial features must be broken down in some way which will allow an efficient explanation of these thirty-four terms and many others. Nevertheless, because of space limitations and because of the arbitrariness of this particular set of synonyms, we will not attempt such a Herculean task.

PERCEPTION FEATURES:

Many readers may have noticed that in the treatment of predicate features, modals were not mentioned. The reason is that modals are extremely subjective and open to individual interpretation. They are, in other words, controlled by the particular perceptions of the speaker and listener, and it is not at all inconsistent if one person says, "You should have been to class on time," and the other person retorts, "No, I should have been where I was—watching the Super Bowl on television." Both of these statements can be true in the sense that they both reflect the value system of the respective speaker. The fact that language purists have not been able to keep or enforce a distinction between *can* and *may* relates to this difference of interpretation as illustrated in the old joke about the school teacher who won't let children go to the bathroom until they say, "May I . . ." instead of the more common, "Can I . . .".

Perception features are individual and subjective and connotative, as opposed to denotative. They are not open to empirical investigation. However we can examine these features and discuss their nature. First we will consider those perception features associated with the modal auxiliaries. The modal auxiliaries signal three basic semantic concepts, all mainly perceptual in nature. These three concepts are (1) Obligation; (2) Reality; and (3) Logical Inference. For each of these there is a range, which can be illustrated as follows:

1. Obligation
   a. Ability
   b. Permission
   c. Obligement
   d. Necessity

2. Reality
    a. Possibility
    b. Probability
    c. Conditionality
    d. Fact

3. Logical Inference
    a. Logical necessity
    b. Logical possibility

It should be noted that obligation and reality refer to the future, at least in the way we have used the terms, while logical inference refers to the past. Also it should be noted that certain of the points in these three ranges logically entail prior points on the range. Thus permission makes no sense unless ability is assumed, and something is not probable unless it is also possible. Further entailments of this type can be seen by illustrating the various points on the three ranges above with actual lexical items. When modality is treated in a system in which semantics is central, words are grouped according to their semantic features, and therefore the part of speech of the various words takes on a much lower level of significance. So, although it looks strange, in the groupings below no attempt is made to distinguish between the modal auxiliary *might,* the regular verb *hope,* and the adjective *inclined* since the only consideration at this particular time is that all three of these words have the perception feature of possibility. The chart that follows is an oversimplification because there is obviously much overlapping.

PERCEPTION FEATURE:	EXAMPLES:
ABILITY	can, be able to, have the ability to, etc.
PERMISSION	may, be permitted to, can, etc.
OBLIGEMENT	should, ought to, be obligated to, be obliged to, etc.
NECESSITY	must, need to, have to, etc.
POSSIBILITY	may, might, be inclined to, be possible, want, hope, etc.

PROBABILITY	expect, suppose, etc.
CONDITIONALITY	should, could, any cause-effect construction, etc.
FACT	shall, will, be going to, must, etc.

LOGICAL NECESSITY	must have, etc.
LOGICAL POSSIBILITY	may have, might have, could have, etc.

But even in languages like English, which happens to have modal auxiliaries, this is by no means the only place where perception features are signaled. In the chart above, there are nouns, e.g., *ability,* verbs, e.g., *expect,* adjectives, e.g., *possible,* past participles, e.g., *obligated,* etc. Consider verbs, for example, which indicate that someone is influenced to do something. Again, there is a range, depending on the amount of force exerted, as follows:

1. Allowance
2. Aid
3. Encouragement
4. Expectation
5. Force

It is possible to give numerous examples of expressions, this time all verbs, which express these five perception features, as follows:

PERCEPTION FEATURE:	EXAMPLES:
ALLOWANCE	allow, appoint, authorize, call on, challenge, choose, commission, dare, elect, employ, empower, enable, engage, entitle, hire, let, license, name, nominate, permit, privilege, tell, write, etc.
AID	aid, assist, coach, demonstrate, design, help, lead, prepare, remind, show, teach, train, etc.

ENCOURAGEMENT	admonish, advise, appeal to, arouse, ask, beg, beseech, communicate, counsel, direct, encourage, enjoin, entreat, exhilarate, exhort, fire up, goad, induce, inspire, instruct, invite, persuade, plead, prompt, provoke, request, say to, stimulate, stir, tempt. urge, warn, etc.
EXPECTATION	count on, desire, expect, intend, (would) like, look for, mean for, prefer, seek for, trust, want, etc.
FORCE	assign, cause, coerce, command, compel, consign, force, get, incite, make, oblige, order, require, etc.

There is an obvious semantic similarity between these classes of verbs and the classes of modals just discussed.

It is also very common for nouns to contain subjective perception features which different speakers will interpret in different ways. Below are some sets of words which share a common denotative feature, but which have many different perception features.

woman	brilliance	bosom	fag
lady	intelligence	breast	dandy
female	smartness	chest	gaffer
bitch	common sense	bust	brute
slut		tits	beast
floozy		boobs	
wench			

It is obvious that in order to measure words like the above, there is a need for tests such as Osgood's, which were described in Chapter III under "Semantic Differentiation."

Adjectives and adverbs demonstrate the same type of difference in perception features. It may be possible to rank them in relation to each other on a particular scale, such as formality, frequency, or evaluation, but it is still not possible to assign precise values to these terms since they are so subjective. In the examples given below, the first column contains adjectives ranked from formal to informal, the second column contains adverbs of frequency ranked from often to seldom, and the last column contains evaluative adjectives ranked from good to bad.

intoxicated	always	tremendous
drunk	often	excellent
tipsy	usually	good
plastered	periodically	ordinary
stoned	sometimes	fair
bombed out	once in a while	poor
	infrequently	awful
	seldom	terrible
	rarely	
	never	

One of the reasons that it is so difficult to assign definite meanings to these words is that *rarely* for one predication might be *often* for another. And even for the same real-world situation one person might describe something as happening *rarely* while because of different experiences and expectations another feels that the same thing happens *often*. Similarly, with general evaluation terms the same item might be labeled *tremendous* by one individual and *poor* by another, depending on the standards of the judge. Adverbs such as *very, too, extremely, awfully,* and *enough* contain very subjective perception features. *Enough* for one person may not be *enough* for another, and even for the same person *enough* of something at one time in his life may not be *enough* or may be *too much* of this thing at another time in his life.

But this vagueness which is a part of all perception features, does not make them any the less interesting or significant to linguists. To a large extent, linguistics is a psychological and social science, reflecting individual and group attitudes and beliefs. Any linguist attempting to give an accurate picture of the semantics of a language cannot afford to ignore these features of perception.

There are a number of other concepts that might possibly be dealt with by an adequate system of semantic features. In Chapter III, we mentioned presupposition and entailment. Possibly these facts could be expressed in terms of semantic features, but there are a great many variables which would have to be taken into consideration.

Another concept which might be described through semantic features is logical transitivity. The meaning of this term, which comes from logic, is very different from the "transitive" used by grammarians. A transitive expression in the logical definition is one which indicates a necessary extension of a logical property such as time or space. Such terms as *precede* and *follow* indicate such an extension. If John precedes Mary, and if Mary precedes Fred, then it must be true that John precedes Fred in either space or time. The most obvious kind of transitive system is that of natural numbers such as 1, 2, 3, 4, or 1st, 2nd, 3rd, and 4th. And such expressions as *more than, less than,* and *fewer than,* also relate items transitively. Another important system of language for which transitivity is a necessary feature is the kinship system. This system is full of transitive concepts. For example, if John is Mary's descendant, and Mary is Bill's descendant, then John must be Bill's descendant. The kinship system is a good example of the way words can be systematically related to each other through a number of different features. For example, kinship terms indicate time as in *great grandfather, grandfather, father, self, son, grandson, great grandson,* etc. They indicate consanguinity as in *brother, sister, sibling,* etc. Some of them indicate sex as in *uncle,* vs. *aunt, son* vs. *daughter, nephew* vs. *niece,* etc. And they also indicate non-blood relationship as *daughter-in-law, stepfather,* etc. All of these types of features, and perhaps others as well, must be taken into account in an adequate description of a kinship system.

In conclusion, although semantic features are extremely complex, they must be directly dealt with because it is through semantic features that we can determine how closely various lexical items are related to each other. The compatibility of two lexical items is a function of the compatibility of the features of these two items. Language acquisition, either first or second, can be expressed in terms of semantic features because in the acquisition of a new language it is often the case that a person knows almost, but not quite, all the features of a particular word or expression. Metaphor can also be explained in terms of semantic features. Personification, for example, is merely the insertion of a particular semantic feature, [+human], into a lexical item. Lexical ambiguity and semantic anomaly and degrees of grammaticality or acceptability also might rely on semantic features for their explanations. And translation from one language or dialect into another can be efficiently accomplished when a person is aware of semantic features common to the two languages which might be under consideration. Semantic features are also necessary in accounting for semantic change, since a word usually changes one feature at a time as new meanings evolve. For example, a word in the United States that is presently undergoing a change in meaning is the word *blackboard*. A hundred years ago this simply meant a wood board painted black. Then as technology changed, blackboards were made from other substances. The feature [+wood] was no longer a part of their lexical meaning, but they were still black surfaces used in school rooms where they were written on with chalk. Today blackboards are seldom black; they are green or brown or even white (for blue chalk). This means that the feature [+black] has changed, but the features concerning use and location etc. remain the same.

Semantic features are necessary to explain many of the facts about deep cases and the relationships between case frames of predicates and semantic categories. They can also help to explain facts about synonymy and paraphrase, and antonymy. But all these issues will be discussed in detail later. It is sufficient to say at this point that semantic features are a necessity, not a luxury, for any person attempting to get at the basis of meaning.

VI. Semantic Cases or Logical Arguments

LOGICAL ARGUMENTS:

Consider the following six sentences in which the verbs are italicized.

1. John *is tall.*
2. John *kissed* Mary.
3. John *gave* Mary a motorcycle.
4. John *made* a motorcyle out of junk with his bare hands.
5. John *bought* a motorcycle for Mary from Bill with $500.
6. John *transported* Mary from Iowa City to Ames via
   Cedar Falls on a motorcycle.

The differences in these sentences can not be due to the subjects since the subjects are all the same, *John.* Rather than the noun being the important part of a sentence, it is usually the verb which is basic and which holds the sentence together both syntactically and semantically. But in sentence (1) the verb *is* somehow doesn't seem to be as important as the other sentences' verbs, i.e., *kissed, gave, made, bought,* and *transported.* In some languages a linking verb like *is* would not be needed so that sentence (1) would be represented as

"John tall." This sounds very non-English because we rely on *is* to do many things. In this sentence, it indicates tense which is present, person which is third, number which is singular, mood which is indicative, and perhaps voice which is active. But these are all grammatical, not semantic, functions. Because of the fact that *is,* whether acting as a main verb or an auxiliary verb, has basically a grammatical function, we will not consider it the predicator. Instead we will think of the word *tall* as the predicator in sentence (1). *John* is the subject or topic of the sentence, and *tall* is what is said, i.e., it is a description about the subject.

If we now extract the simple predicate from the five sentences above, we will get *tall* or *is tall, kissed, gave, made, bought,* and *transported.* We will call these units the verbs of their respective sentences. Although the verb is the most important single part of the sentence, it is usually accompanied by other units, except in special cases such as the idiom, "It's raining." These units which accompany the verb can be called logical arguments. These arguments generally appear as nouns or noun phrases in English sentences. For easy reference, let us assign an arbitrary letter of the alphabet to each of the noun expressions in sentences one through six, as follows:

> q John
> r Mary
> s a motorcycle
> t junk
> u bare hands
> v Bill
> w $500
> x Iowa City
> y Ames
> z Cedar Falls

Now, if we represent the six sentences under consideration by the non-inflected verb followed by the marking for the particular nouns that go with this verb, the following pattern emerges:

> 1. $tall_q$
> 2. $kiss_{q\ r}$
> 3. $give_{q\ r\ s}$
> 4. $make_{q\ s\ t\ u}$

5. buy$_{q\ s\ r\ v\ w}$
6. transport$_{q\ r\ x\ y\ z\ s}$

Sentence (1), "John is tall," has only one noun associated with the verb; it is therefore called a one-place predicate. Sentence (2), "John kissed Mary," has two nouns associated with the verb, and is therefore a two-place predicate. Sentence (3), "John gave Mary a motorcycle," is a three-place predicate; sentence (4), "John made a motorcycle out of junk with his bare hands," is a four-place predicate; sentence (5), "John bought a motorcycle for Mary from Bill with $500," is a five-place predicate; and finally sentence (6), "John transported Mary from Iowa City to Ames via Cedar Falls on a motorcycle," is a six-place predicate.

FUNCTIONAL RELATIONSHIPS:

This information about arguments is essential. Probably the single most important thing we can know about a verb is how many arguments are associated with it. But in addition to this quantitative question, we must also ask a qualitative question. In other words, we must know not only how many arguments are associated with a particular verb, but also what types of arguments they are. We will begin the investigation of the types of arguments by considering such concepts as subject, direct object, indirect object, object complement, and object of preposition. It can be seen from our six examples that the subject comes before the verb and agrees with a present tense verb in number and person, while the various kinds of objects all come after the verb in a normal English sentence. Furthermore, it can be seen that all these sentences have a subject; that all but (1) have a direct object; that all but (1) and (2) have not only a subject and a direct object, but other kinds of objects as well, increasing in number from sentences (3) to (6). Based on this information, we could say that sentence (1) is intransitive, sentence (2) is transitive, sentence (3) is a special kind of transitive that takes an indirect object, etc.

On the basis of this type of information, sentences have been classified according to the number and kinds of non-prepositional noun phrases that follow the verb, in somewhat the following way:

CLASS:	STRUCTURE:	EXAMPLE:
I	NP V	John golfs.
II	NP_1 V NP_2	John kissed Mary.
III	NP_1 V NP_1	John is a farmer.
IV	NP_1 V NP_2 NP_3	John gave Mary a kiss.
V	NP_1 V NP_2 NP_2	We elected John president.

Although many linguists have proposed various sub-classes of these major sentence types, most would agree that these are the five basic types. However, some would describe them differently by noting the function rather than the part of speech. In this alternate kind of description the classes of sentences would be described as follows:

CLASS:	STRUCTURE:	EXAMPLE:
I	Subject Predicate	John golfs.
II	Subject Predicate Direct-Object	John kissed Mary.
III	Subject Predicate Subjective-Complement	John is a farmer.
IV	Subject Predicate Indirect-Object Direct-Object	John gave Mary a kiss.
V	Subject Predicate Direct-Object Object-Complement	We elected John president.

Such a classification is determined by the number and the type of complements which follow the verb. This type of sentence classification is perfectly valid and would be a necessary part of the description of any particular language similar to English. But this classification has one important limitation. Because it is syntactically motivated, it is to some extent different for each particular language, and again, because of the syntactic bias, there is no separate consideration of the different kinds of prepositional phrases and variations in such structures as subjects and direct objects.

DEEP CASES:

But now let us consider a third type of sentence analysis. This type combines the information of the first classification, which is according to quantity, with that of the second classification, which is according to syntactic quality, and it takes into consideration the semantic quality as well. This type of sentence classification will rely on the interrelationships of deep cases in a sentence. First, let us label each of the noun phrases of the six sentences under consideration at the beginning of this chapter, according to the precise role it plays in its respective sentence. When we do this, the prepositions become helpful in identifying these roles which are called "deep cases." For example, *out of junk* can be identified as a Source partially because of the preposition *out.* In the same way, *with his bare hands,* can be identified as Instrument, *for Mary* as Experiencer, *from Bill* as Source, *with $500* as Instrument or Amount, *from Iowa City* as Source, *to Ames* as Goal, *via Cedar Falls* as Path, and *on a motorcycle* as Instrument. The prepositions are a helpful, but superficial, aid in determining case assignments. In our six sentences, for example, both *out of* and *from* mark a Source. Furthermore, there are many noun expressions in English which are not marked by any prepositions at all, for example in the sample sentences (1)-(5) *John, Mary,* and *motorcycle* have no prepositions, yet these nouns must also be assigned to a particular deep case. Deep cases can be considered bundles of features of the following sort:

> Agent: [+Animate] [+Cause]
> Instrument: [−Animate] [+Cause] [+Receiver]
> Experiencer: [+Animate] [+Receiver]
> Object: [−Animate] [+Receiver]
> Source: [+Origin]
> Path: [+Intermediate State or Position]
> Goal: [+Result]

By using these cases it is now possible to give a more precise analysis of the six verbs, as follows:

1. *tall:* Object
2. *kiss:* Agent, Object
3. *give:* Agent, Experiencer, Object
4. *make:* Agent, Object, Source, Instrument
5. *buy:* Agent, Object, Experiencer, Source, Instrument
6. *transport:* Agent, Object, Source, Goal, Path, Instrument

The identification of the cases which fit with these particular verbs makes it possible to write their case frames. Again, we should say that *tall* is a one-place predicate, that *kiss* is a two-place predicate, and so on, but now we can be more precise about the nature of these various places as follows:

VERB:	CASE FRAME:
tall	$[----+ O]$
kiss	$[----+ A, O]$
give	$[----+ A, E, O]$
make	$[----+ A, O, (S), (I)]$
buy	$[----+ A, O, (E), (S), (I)]$
transport	$[----+ A, O, (S), (G), (P), (I)]$

Notice that parentheses are placed around all of those cases (or arguments) which appear in English surface structure as prepositional phrases. This is because prepositional phrases can be deleted in the surface structure of English, and the resulting sentence will still be grammatical, even though it is not as semantically complete. It should be stressed, however, that deleting these arguments from the surface structure does not delete them from the deep structure. For example, the sentence, "John transported the children," is a six-place predicate, even though only two of the arguments have reached the surface. It is impossible to say the sentence, "John transported the children," without somehow realizing that they went from a certain place (Source), to a certain place (Goal), by way of certain points (Path), in a particular type of vehicle (Instrument).

These deep cases which have been considered so far are controlled by the verb. There are some other cases, however, that are possible in almost any sentence, such as expressions of Time, Place, or Manner. Such expressions as *yesterday, in the state of Delaware,* and *hesitantly* are appropriate for all the six sentences under consideration which have an active, as opposed to stative, verb. Because these expressions can go with such a large number of divergent sentences, they are not considered as either belonging or not belonging to the case frame of a particular verb, but instead are associated with the major class of verbs identified as active. Furthermore, these last three cases (Time, Place, and Manner) modify the entire sentence in a way which the other cases (Agent, Instrument, Experiencer, Object, Source, Path, and Goal) do not. The following diagram represents this dichotomy bytween Adverbial cases, which Fillmore called Modal cases, and Propositional cases:

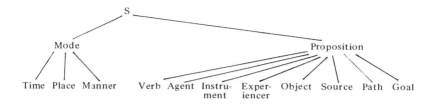

There is obviously a relationship between these deep cases and sentence functions such as subject and direct object. In fact, it is possible to say that the subject of a sentence is usually an Agent, that the indirect object of a sentence is usually an Experiencer, and that the direct object of a sentence is usually an Object, but consider such a sentence as, "John received a letter in the mail." In this sentence, *John* is certainly not the Agent, i.e., the animate cause. We must be very careful to stress that there is only a loose relationship between deep cases and sentence function since in English it is possible for any deep case to occur as the subject, as the direct object, or as the object of a preposition as the following sentences illustrate:

AGENT:
    as Subject: *John* went from Iowa City to Des Moines.
    as Direct Object: Highway 80 took *John* from Iowa City to Des Moines.
    as Object of Prep: This route was first taken by *John.*

INSTRUMENT:
    as Subject: This *ax* will cut plastic.
    as Direct Object: He bought *an ax* yesterday.
    as Object of Prep: He damaged the carton with *his new ax.*

BODY PART:
    as Subject: *His foot* slipped.
    as Direct Object: He used *his teeth* to puncture the balloon.
    as Object of Prep.: He punctured the balloon with *his teeth.*

FORCE:
    as Subject: *A bolt of lightning* destroyed the tree.
    as Direct Object: Zeus used *a bolt of lightning* to destroy the tree.
    as Object of Prep.: Zeus destroyed the tree with *a bolt of lightning.*

MATERIAL:
    as Subject: *Silt* should not be used in making cement.
    as Direct Object: They used *silt* when they made the cement.
    as Object of Prep.: They made cement out of *silt* and some other stuff.

EXPERIENCER:
    as Subject: *John* enjoyed the spectacle.
    as Direct Object: The spectacle amused *John.*
    as Object of Prep.: The spectacle was very enjoyable to *John.*

OBJECT:
    as Subject: *The window* suddenly shattered.
    as Direct Object: John suddenly shattered *the window.*
    as Object of Prep.: The floor was covered with *shattered window glass.*

MANNER:
    as Subject: *His savoir-faire* sometimes amazes me.
    as Direct Object: He seems to exude *savoir-faire.*
    as Object of Prep.: She minimized the misunderstanding with *savoir-faire.*

EXTENT:
    as Subject: *$100* will buy a fairly decent record player.
    as Direct Object: This typewriter cost *$200.*
    as Object of Prep.: John bought a radio for *$15.*

REASON:
    as Subject: *John's inability to concentrate* caused him to fail
                      the course

    as Direct Object: The teacher used *John's tardiness* as an excuse to
                      fail him.

    as Object of Prep.: Mary passed the course by *being on time* and by
                      concentrating on the lesson.

LOCATIVE:
    as Subject: *Phoenix* is beautiful this time of year.
    as Direct Object: I like *Kalamazoo* more than Raleigh.
    as Object of Prep.: I spent last summer in *Bloomington.*

TEMPORAL:
    as Subject: *6:00 A.M.* comes much too early for me.
    as Direct Object: John dislikes *all of the winter months.*
    as Object of Prep.: John won't have to work so hard after *the*
                      Christmas season.

SOURCE:
 as Subject: *John* sold Mary his bicycle.
 as Direct Object: John left *Nepal* because of political pressure.
 as Object of Prep.: The defensive center intercepted a pass from *the offensive fullback.*

PATH:
 as Subject: *Detroit* was his first layover.
 as Direct Object: He bypassed *Spanish Fork* on his trip from Payson to Salt Lake City.
 as Object of Prep.: He went by way of *Norman, Oklahoma.*

GOAL:
 as Subject: *John* received a "dear John" letter from Mary.
 as Direct Object: Mary saw *John* the next day.
 as Object of Prep.: Mary sent her hotel key to *John.*

From these examples, it can be seen that any deep case can occur either as a subject, as a direct object, or as the object of a preposition. This is possible because such concepts as Agent, Object, and Experiencer are deep cases with semantic (deep structure) justification while subject, direct object, indirect object, etc. are surface functions with syntactic (surface structure) justification. The deep cases such as Agent are universals; they occur in all natural languages. But the surface functions such as subject are very different from language to language. This is not to imply, however, that these surface functions do not play an important role in language. For example, it is on the basis of such surface considerations that agreement is determined. In English, for example, a verb agrees in person and number with its subject, not with its Agent. Compare the sentence, "The boys *are* hitting Mary," with its paraphrase, "Mary *is* being hit by the boys." In both of these sentences, *the boys,* is the Agent and *Mary* is the Experiencer. If a verb agreed with the Agent, it would be plural in both sentences since the Agent (*the boys*) is plural in both sentences. But Agent is a concept of deep structure; and subject-verb agreement, along with other kinds of agreement, is determined by surface functions rather than by deep structure considerations.

 Surface functions also indicate the distribution of old and new information. In the sentence, "The boys are hitting Mary," the predication is the most important part of the communication. The subject of the sentence, *The boys,* is the topic or the theme of the sentence; it can be thought of as the old information. The predication of the sentence, *are hitting Mary,* is the comment or the rheme of the sentence; it can be thought of as the new information. In the passive sentence, "Mary is being hit by the boys," *Mary* becomes the subject of the sentence even though she is still the Experiencer. This means that in the passive sentence, *Mary* is the topic or theme or old information, and *is being hit by the boys* is the complete predicate and is therefore the comment, or rheme, or new information. This shows us that the distribution of old and new information is a function of surface structure considerations such as subject, object of preposition, etc., rather than deep structure considerations such as Agent, Experiencer, etc.

A third important role filled by surface functions is to indicate which noun phrases have a freedom of movement, or a freedom of deletion. It has already been demonstrated that any deep case can reach English surface structure as a subject, as a direct object, or as the object of a preposition. If a person were to go back over these examples, or any standard English sentences for that matter, he would find that the deletion of the subjects or deletion of the direct objects would result in ungrammatical sentences, though an exception to this generalization is that direct objects can be deleted from pseudo-intransitive verbs so that both "I ate a banana this morning," and "I ate __∅__ this morning," are grammatical. While subjects and direct objects can usually not be deleted, prepositional phrases usually *can* be. Any speaker or writer of the language has the option of making a particular noun phrase the subject, direct object, or object of a preposition in a sentence. If he chooses to make it an object of a preposition, he can move it around in the sentence for special effects, or can, in fact, delete it altogether. To illustrate this point, let us reconsider the Force case. When the Force appears as the subject as in, "*A bolt of lightning* destroyed the tree," or as the direct object as in "Zeus used *a bolt of lightning* to destroy the tree," it cannot be deleted from the sentence. But this same Force when it appears as the object of a preposition, as in "Zeus destroyed the tree with *a bolt of lightning,*" can be moved around in the sentence to result in, "With *a bolt of lightning,* Zeus destroyed the tree," "Zeus, with *a bolt of lightning,* destroyed the tree," or possibly even, "Zeus destroyed, with *a bolt of lightning,* the tree." And, again, when the noun phrase in question appears as the object of a preposition, it can be deleted altogether without making the sentence ungrammatical, as in "Zeus destroyed the tree."

It is interesting that the nondeletable functions of subject and direct object are normally positioned immediately next to the verb. It brings about a special effect or unusual emphasis when words or phrases are placed between the subject, verb, and direct object, as they were in some of the above examples about Zeus and the lightning. In English the normal subject position is immediately before the verb, and the normal direct object position is immediately following the verb. Even objective complements and indirect objects come as close to the verb as they can. Prepositional phrases generally occupy positions at the extreme locations, either the beginnings or the ends of sentences. This clustering of nondeletable items around the verb seems to be a fact not only in English but in Indo-European languages in general, as well as in many other unrelated languages. It may even be a universal tendency that the verb, as the most significant part of the predication, serves as a magnet drawing close to itself the nondeletable elements.

INTERRELATIONSHIPS AMONG DEEP CASES:

Earlier in this chapter we mentioned that deep cases can be thought of as bundles of semantic features. We indicated that Agent had the features [+Animate] and [+Cause]; and that Experiencer had the features [+Animate] and [+Receiver]. If the term Agent is nothing more than a short-cut way of saying Animate Cause, a logical question to ask is whether it simplifies or complicates the grammar to have this intermediate level of deep cases in addition to features. The question is whether or not it would be possible to just identify the features and forget about deep cases. This problem is not yet resolved. First, it may be true that the human mind can benefit from this intermediate, perhaps redundant, level of deep case even though, for efficiency it would be best disposed of in computer programs. Second, it is not clear that this level of deep cases is totally redundant. One fact which is relevant to this issue is that deep cases represent a relationship between inherent features, like animate, and relational features, like cause. Consider the four deep cases, Agent,

Experiencer, Instrument, and Object, in terms of their inherent features and relational features:

DEEP CASE:	INHERENT FEATURE:	RELATIONAL FEATURE:
Agent	Animate	Cause
Experiencer	Animate	Effect
Instrument	Inanimate	Cause
Object	Inanimate	Effect

These four cases, then, can be described in terms of two feature dichotomies: animate-inanimate and cause-effect. Furthermore, we can begin to see similarities and differences between these four cases. Agents and Experiencers are both animate, while Instruments and Objects are both inanimate. Agents and Instruments are both causes, while Experiencers and Objects are both effects. Since the features animate and cause are basically active features, while the features inanimate and effect are basically passive features, we can now explain that the Agent is most eligible to become the subject of a sentence because it consists entirely of active features and the subject position in English, and many other languages, is normally the position for the most active case. The direct object position in English, and in many other languages, is normally the position for the least active case. This is why the Object with its all-passive features is most eligible to become a direct object while an Agent with its all-active features is least eligible for this position. On the other hand, Instruments and Experiencers are equally comfortable as subjects or direct objects because they are partly active and partly passive in nature.

In the last paragraph it was shown that deep cases are not merely bundles of features but that in addition there is some relationship between deep cases (Agent, Experiencer, Object, etc.) and grammatical functions (subject, indirect object, direct object, etc.). For a long time, grammarians have been attempting to investigate the interrelationships among the various grammatical functions. They have noted that except for imperative sentences, all English sentences have a surface subject, even if this surface subject sometimes takes the form of an expletive as in, *"There* are many suicides in late winter," or *"It* is difficult to understand how he did that." They have further noted that it is impossible to have an indirect object or an objective complement without having a direct object. And they have noted that a transitive verb somehow carries the action from the subject (actor) to the direct object (receiver of the action), while an intransitive verb merely indicates the action of the subject, and a linking verb indicates a modificational or restrictive relationship between the subject and the subjective complement. All of these relationships between various functions within a sentence are highly significant in explaining how the grammar of a particular language such as English functions. But let us now turn to the relationships which hold among the various deep cases. These relationships hold regardless of the particular language being discussed, because they are universal relationships. Consider the following seven sentences:

OBJECT
John is tall.

AGENT
John snores.

FORCE
The wind howled.

FORCE   OBJECT
An earthquake destroyed *the city.*

AGENT EXP OBJECT
Mary gave *John her heart.*

AGENT OBJECT INSTRUMENT
John broke *the window* (with *a hammer*).

AGENT GOAL SOURCE
John built *a castle* (out of *sand*).

AGENT   SOURCE   GOAL   PATH
John cycled (from *San Francisco*) (to *Berkeley*) (via the *Golden Gate Bridge*).

There are three deep cases which are totally autonomous: Object, Agent, and Force. These three cases can occur alone in a sentence without implying the presence of any other case even in the deep structure. The Object case can occur alone only with stative verbs, as in "John is tall." The Agent and Force cases, on the other hand, occur only with action verbs, as in "John snores," or "The wind howled." The reason that *John* is an Object in *"John* is tall," and an Agent in, *"John* snores," is that in the latter sentence John is doing something. *Snoring* is an action while *being tall* is a state. All of the deep cases except Object, Agent, and Force are dependent on other cases for their existence. It might even be argued that *John* in "John is tall," is sufficiently different from *the city* in, "An earthquake destroyed the city," to be classed as something other than an Object. If this is done, then even the Object case is dependent on some other deep case for its existence. Now consider *John* in the sentence, "Mary gave John her heart." Here *John* is an Experiencer. It would be difficult to think of an Experiencer which didn't have an Object to experience at least in the deep structure. It may be that the object does not come through an agent as is true in the sentences, "John enjoys the forest," or "The darkness frightened John," but still *the forest* and *the darkness* are Objects being Experienced by John.

The Instrumental case exhibits an even more complex interrelationship with the other cases. Earlier we defined the Instrument as the inanimate cause. It must therefore have an Object, since the Object is affected by the Instrument. In this cause-effect relationship, therefore, it is the Instrument which is the cause and the Object which is affected. But this is not the whole story. At the same time that the Instrument has some effect over the Object, the Agent has some effect over the Instrument. A sentence like, "John broke the window with a hammer," could be paraphrased as "John caused a hammer to cause the window to break." So *a hammer* (the Instrument) is controlled by *John* (the Agent), and affects *the window* (the Object). In the sentence, "A hammer broke the window," this analysis is no less true, even though only the last part of the chain of causation is present in the surface structure. The sentence, "A hammer broke the window," has two possible interpretations. One is that the hammer was controlled by an Agent (or possibly a Force), and this Agent did not reach the surface structure. In this case, "A hammer broke the window," is a paraphrase of "John broke the window with a hammer." The other interpretation is metaphorical and involves personificiation, or at least "animation" of *a hammer.* In the second case, *a hammer* is not in Instrument but is rather a metaphorical Agent.

Now let us consider Source, Path, and Goal. In the first place, it should be pointed out that these three cases occur only with action verbs and that action verbs require Agents. So Source, Path, and Goal can occur only in sentences with Agents, at least in the deep structure. Since deep cases must be defined in a very abstract way, the concepts of Source, Path, and Goal are relevant not only for changes of state, but also for changes of location, time, etc. As examples of change of state, consider the following three sentences:

> The tailor altered the suit.
> The tailor destroyed the suit.
> The tailor made the suit.

In each of these sentences there is an Agent, *the tailor,* and something else, *the suit.* In the sentence, "The tailor destroyed the suit," *the suit* is the Source and the unstated Goal is the shreds or ashes that the suit became. In the sentence, "The tailor made the suit," *the suit* is the Goal and the unstated Source is the material, thread, buttons, zipper, etc. out of which the suit was made. In the sentence, "The tailor altered the suit," *the suit* is both the Source and the Goal, but it is a different suit. *The suit* which is the Source is the suit as it existed *before* alteration; *the suit* which is the Goal is the suit as it existed *after* alteration. With change-of-state verbs it is not always easy to conceive of a Path; however, it is always there, and it represents the item in transition from the Source state to the Goal state. With locative and temporal verbs, the Path is more obvious. When a person says, "I went from Chicago to Phoenix," he must have taken a certain path to make this journey, even though this path does not need to be stated explicitly. When a person says, "I studied from 8:00 A.M. till 9:00 A.M.," again it implies a Path leading from 8:00 A.M. going to 9:00 A.M. and passing through the temporal points 8:01, 8:02, 8:03, etc. So the point we are trying to make is that the cases Source, Path, and Goal are totally dependent upon each other, whether these represent states, times, locations, etc.

The Object case is the least understood of the deep cases, and in fact, at one time this was considered the case to use for those examples which could not be neatly classified as something else. One of the important functions of the Object case is to indicate transitivity. *Bring* and *take* are actually the transitive counterparts of *come* and *go.* As transitive verbs, the first set takes an Object in the surface structure while the second set does not. But as a matter of fact, the second set might also be conceived of as having an Object in the deep structure that is deleted in the surface structure, because these "intransitive" verbs merely indicate that the subject and direct object are identical. This is why the sentence, "John came home," means the same as *"John brought himself home." This notion will be discussed further in the next chapter.

There are few restrictions on the adverbial cases. They usually occur in sentences with action verbs and therefore with Agents in the deep structure. Locative, Temporal, Manner, Extent, Reason, etc. are possible, but not necessary, for any kind of active verb. This means that they have an extremely loose relationship with the other deep cases.

VII. Semantic Categories and the Case Frames of Predicates

There are two facts about deep cases which make them highly significant. First, they are semantically justified and therefore have a relationship with the real world of experience. Second, they are universal in nature; such concepts as Agent, Instrument, Experiencer, Object, Source, Path, Goal, Time, Place, Manner, Extent, Reason, etc. are equally significant in Hungarian (a Finno-Ugric language), Arabic (a Semitic language), Mandarin Chinese (a Sino-Tibetan language), Swahili (a Bantu language), Persian (an Indo-European language), etc. From a semantic point of view, it is of little significance that these cases may be marked by such things as prepositions, affixes, and/or word order in different languages and that even in the same language the marking system may change, as in English where *John* is the Agent whether it occurs with a preposition as in, "The cake was eaten by *John,*" or without a preposition as in, *"John* ate the cake." In fact, because deep cases are semantically justified, they can be identified regardless of their surface structure markings and regardless of the particular language under consideration.

Since deep cases are semantically justifiable and since they are linguistically universal, it is perfectly reasonable to assume that all verbs which represent a particular semantic area in the real world would have exactly the same case frame as all other words in this same semantic area and that there would therefore be a perfect positive correlation between semantic categories and case frames of verbs; and furthermore that this relationship between semantic area and case frame applies across language boundaries. Any verb of contact, for example English *to hit*, would have an Agent, an Instrument, and an Object in the deep structure of any human language. A verb of perception, for example English *to enjoy* would have an Experiencer and an Object in the deep structure of any human language. Limitations of space will not allow us to develop this universal notion by treating a large number of languages in depth. Therefore we will only consider English in depth, but as you read this, try to envision in your mind the situation in other languages with which you happen to be familiar. We are confident that you will conclude that the statements which are being made about English will apply equally well to other languages. And although you may not be able to think of direct translations of some of the English words into a particular language, no doubt there are translation paraphrases of *all* the English expressions. And again, whatever is said about the semantics or the case frames of the English examples, will also be true of the paraphrases in other languages.

In order to keep from being inundated by the numerous details to be presented in this chapter, we will begin by presenting an outline of semantic categories of verbs. We will then discuss the categories and correlate them with case frames.

I.   One-Place Predicates
   A.   Description (e.g., *to be cold*)
   B.   Action (e.g., *to be careful*)
   C.   Sound (e.g., *to snap*)

II. Verbs of Motion
   A.   Transportation (e.g., *to walk*)
   B.   Transfer (e.g., *to throw*)
   C.   Exchange (e.g., *to reimburse*)
   D.   Communication (e.g., *to explain*)

III. Verbs of Location
   A.   Containment (e.g., *to bottle*)
   B.   Attachment (e.g., *to button*)

C. Enclosure (e.g., *to screen in*)

D. Covering (e.g., *to asphalt*)

IV. Verbs of Contact

A. Contact (e.g., *to hit*)

B. Proximity (e.g., *to pass*)

V. Verbs of Experience

A. Sense (e.g., *to see*)

B. Perception (e.g., *to comprehend*)

C. Psychological Event (e.g., *to enjoy*)

D. Ownership (e.g., *to possess*)

VI. Verbs of Change

A. Alteration (e.g., *to brighten*)

B. Creation (e.g., *to build*)

C. Destruction

1. Partial Inanimate Destruction (e.g., *to puncture*)

2. Total Inanimate Destruction (e.g., *to demolish*)

3. Partial Animate Destruction (e.g., *to wound*)

4. Total Animate Destruction (e.g., *to decapitate*)

VII. Symmetrical Predicates (e.g., *to resemble*)

VIII. Set Case Frame (e.g., *to co-author*)

As each of these major semantic classes of verbs is discussed, two things should be noticed. First, even though each of these semantic classes contains a very large number of individual verbs, the verbs of each semantic class all have exactly the same case frame. And second, verbs of this same semantic class have exactly the same case frame, regardless of what particular language they happen to represent.

ONE PLACE PREDICATES:

We will begin with an oversimplification by saying that single-place predicates in a semantically oriented model would probably include two of the categories of traditional and structural grammar—intransitive verbs and linking verbs. Intransitive verbs are one-place predicates because they have nothing more than a subject. Linking verbs are one-place predicates because the subjective complement is now thought of as the verb itself, so here also there is only one accompanying argument or case. This is an oversimplified statement of relationship because the traditional and structural models were basically concerned with surface structure, while semantic models must be basically concerned with deep structure. Therefore the definition of an intransitive verb as a verb that takes no non-prepositional phrase complements is a surface structure definition. But the definition of a single-place predicate as a verb that has only one nonadverbial argument or case associated with it in the underlying deep structure is a deep structure definition. This means that a sentence might have no non-prepositional phrase complements in its surface structure, but still not be a single-place predicate because there might be an argument inherent to the verb which did not reach the surface or which reached the surface as a prepositional phrase.

In talking about one-place predicates, we will first discuss those associated with linking verbs like *be.* And of these, we will first consider descriptive expressions like the following:

advantageous, accidental, alive, ashamed, asleep, dangerous, dead, despondent, elementary, fat, fatal, fortunate, fragile, grateful, impotent, intelligent, latent, miraculous, poor, popular, possible, profitable, red, rich, short, tall, thankful, thin. . . .

Adjectives of this type are extremely common, and the list could be extended almost endlessly. It should be noted that all of these expressions are stative rather than active, and that they usually represent fairly long-lasting states. Weather expressions are similar to the expressions just listed. Among others, they would include the following:

awful, beautiful, cloudy, cold, drizzl(ing), foggy, freez(ing), hail(ing), hot, lovely, miserable, misty, rain(ing), sleet(ing), smog(gy), snow(ing), terrible, warm, windy. . . .

Some of these expressions are used mainly as weather terms, e.g., *cloudy, foggy* and *windy;* others are used to describe things in general, including the weather, e.g., *beautiful, cold,* and *terrible.* The strictly weather expressions represent an extremely limited set, but the more general expressions represent a much larger class. All of the expressions discussed so far in this chapter, including the weather expressions, can be classed as descriptive and in some sense stative. They occur with Objects as the single argument in their case frames. They are all adjectives, though some of these adjectives are derived from verbs like *raining* and *ashamed.* At this point, a person might be tempted to say that all adjectives used as predicates (*predicate adjectives* in traditional terminology) are like those just discussed and have Objects as the single argument of their case frames. This is not the situation, however, because statements like "John is tall," which is simply describing a state rather than an action, differ from something like "John is boring," where *John* is an Agent somehow responsible for doing something. Examples of expressions like this latter kind which take only Agents in their case frames include the following:

> asinine, captain, careful, cautious, discrete, a farmer, foolish, frank, impolite, insistent, nasty, noisy, offensive, officious, persistent, polite, pleasant, realistic, reasonable, reckless, rough, rude, silly, tactful, a teacher, troublesome, unfair, unpleasant, useful....

Some of the subjective complements in this class of "verbs" are nouns rather than adjectives. Consider, for example, the sentence, "John is captain." It would appear that this is a two-place, rather than a one-place predicate, but that may be an incorrect analysis. In support of considering this a one-place predicate, with an Agent as the single case accompanying the verb *captain,* is the fact that to be a captain is to do the things that a captain does. Just as a farmer farms and a teacher teaches, a captain "captains." And if John is a captain, then John does the things that a captain does, whatever they are. But there is also a sense in which, "John is a captain," is a two-place predicate. The verb *to be* can be thought of as exhibiting a part-whole relationship. The set to the left of *be* is a member of the set to the right of *be.* In our example, the one-member set *John* is contained in the many-member set *captains.* Since the set to the left of *be* is always contained in the set to the right of *be,* the set to the left usually represents a smaller class than does the one to the right; therefore it is usually impossible to reverse the two sets. The ungrammaticality of, *"A captain is John," would support this analysis.

It is not surprising that intransitive verbs, as well as subjective complements can be one-place predicates with the Agent (the thing itself) filling that single place. Examples include, *crumble, decay, decompose, disintegrate, fall apart.* . . .

With a set of words incorporating parts of the body, it is difficult to know whether these should be considered one-place predicates or two-place predicates. They appear to be one-place predicates when the body part is totally incorporated. For example, *cry, laugh,* and *weep* incorporate *face; nod* incorporates *head; blink* and *wink* incorporate *eye; frown* and *scowl* incorporate *brow; purse, whistle, smile,* and *grin* incorporate *lips; spit* and *slobber* incorporate *mouth;* and *shrug* incorporates *shoulder.* An alternate interpretation of these words could be that they are two-place predicates with one part not reaching the surface structure because of its being incorporated. This viewpoint would say that it is simply a matter of surface structure peculiarity that with some of these words the body part is not allowed to reach the surface, i.e., *smile, laugh, frown;* with other words it is optional, i.e., *nod (your head), wink (your eye);* while with still others it is obligatory, i.e., *stub your toe, sprain your ankle,* etc.

There are a number of single-place predicates in which this single place is filled by an Instrument. This represents the semantic class of sound and includes the following predicates:

bang, buzz, chime, clang, clank, clatter, click, crack, crackle, crash, creak, ding, gurgle, hum, hiss, pop, roar, rumble, smack, snap, thud, whine, whistle. . . .

In conclusion, either subjective complements or intransitive verbs can be single-place predicates. In general, when a verb represents a state, the deep case that goes with it is an Object; when the verb represents an action the deep case that goes with it is an Agent, and when the verb represents a sound the deep case that goes with it is an Instrument.

We should make one final point before leaving this section. Does a sentence like, "The bishop, his counselors, and most of the members gathered together for the conference," contain three arguments or only one? And what about, "They gathered together for the conference."? Does this second sentence have two fewer arguments than the first even though it refers to the same real-world event? It is probably best to think of such expressions as *gather together, assemble, pair off, numerous,* etc. as one-place predicates in which the one place must be filled by some plural concept, and in which this condition of plurality might be satisfied by conjunction, simple pluralization, or both. More will be said about predicates which require plural arguments in a later section on case frames.

There are a number of verbs which appear to be single-place predicates which actually may not be. Consider the following set of expressions:

> evident, apparent, clear, obvious, a mystery, odd, exciting, obscene, unbelievable, strange. . . .

An Object can be *clear* or *strange,* etc., but so can an action or a state. For that reason it is possible to say "His coming so early was strange," or even, "It was strange for him to come so early." The case frame for such expressions might be merely [———— O], showing that the only case required is Object, but it should be kept in mind that in this situation the Object may be represented by an entire sentence and as such it will have a case frame of its own.

VERBS OF MOTION:

From a mathematical point of view, it might have been best to organize the verbs in this chapter according to the number of arguments required in the predicate. With that organization, we would have first discussed one-place predicates, then two-place predicates, then three-place predicates, and so on. Although such an organization would have been revealing, and although there would have been some correlation between number of predicates and semantic categories, the correlation would not have been a tight one. Since we are focusing on semantics, we decided to use the semantic categories as our principle of organization. From this we will see how well the case frames correlate with these semantic categories rather than the other way around.

Verbs of motion can be broken into four classes: transportation, e.g., *walk;* transfer, e.g., *throw;* exchange, e.g., *reimburse;* and communication, e.g., *explain.* For all four of these verb classes, there is an Object, often not explicitly stated, which begins in one place and ends up in another. It might be argued that the Object for verbs of transportation, transfer, and exchange is very different in nature from the Object for verbs of communication. The Object for the first three classes of verbs is concrete, while the Object for verbs of communication, i.e., that which is communicated—the utterance or speech—is certainly less concrete. A possible solution to this problem would be to say that all four types of verbs belong to the same set, verbs of motion, but that verbs of communication form a different subset from the other three categories. At any rate, let us examine these verbs of motion to determine their function in relation to the real world and their resultant case frames.

Regular verbs of transportation include the following:

ascend, arrive, climb, coast, creep, come, dart, enter, fall, float, fly, go, hurry, jiggle, leave, move, pole, roll, rotate, slide, slither, swim, travel....

These words might be further subcategorized according to whether the movement is up, e.g., *ascend, climb;* or down, e.g., *descend, fall;* according to whether the movement is toward something, e.g., *arrive, enter;* or away from something, e.g., *leave, exit;* or in a circle, e.g., *rotate, revolve;* or according to whether the movement is fast, e.g., *dart, hurry;* or slow, e.g., *creep, crawl.* And very often the word also indicates the types of body contortions and/or the medium through which the movement takes place, e.g., *swim, fly, slither.* It is obvious that such notions as direction, speed, manner, etc. are relevant, regardless of the category of verb under consideration.

Now consider a sentence like, "John went from Miami to New York in an airplane," as compared with, "John flew from Miami to New York." Here the expression *to go in an airplane* is equivalent to the expression *to fly.* In some statements there is nothing in the shape of a particular word to indicate what is being incorporated. The word *fly* incorporates the word *airplane* even though there is no phonetic or orthographic similarity between the words. This is known as opaque lexical incorporation because it is hidden. We can not see in the word itself any traces of the incorporated item. But consider a sentence like, "John went from Miami to New York by bicycle," as compared with, "John (bi)cycled from Miami to New York." In this case the similarity between *go by bicycle* and *(bi)cycle* is obvious, and this is therefore an example of transparent lexical incorporation. The verbs *(bi)cycle, boat, drive, fly, (motor)cycle, navigate, skate, ski,* and *sled* are all examples of transportation verbs in which the Instrument has been incorporated either opaquely or transparently. The Instrument which is probably incorporated into transportation verbs most often is *legs.* Consider the following examples which in their most common usage mean some kind of movement of legs:

> amble, canter, clomp, (tap)dance, dash, dodge, gallop, goosestep, hike, hop, hurdle, jog, jump, leap, limp, lope, march, meander, pedal, prance, prod, promenade, ramble, romp, rove, run, saunter, scamper, skate, ski, skip, sprint, stagger, stalk, step, tramp, tromp, trot, wade, walk, wander....

With these words it is possible to extract additional semantic features. Such expressions as *prance, march, goosestep,* and *promenade* represent a proud kind of movement, while *plod, stagger, limp,* and *trip* represent a tired kind of movement. Such expressions as *hurdle, hop, jump, skip, dodge, leap,* and *step* represent a short-distance move, usually of a single body motion or step, while the other words represent longer distances, with such words as *stalk, jog, plod,* and *march* probably representing very long distances. Whether or not the person moving is thinking about a particular goal location is also a feature of many of these words. Such words as *stalk, jump,* and *dash* are probably toward a particular place, but *meander, saunter,* and *wander* by definition are non-goal oriented. And these three words, plus *amble, stalk,* and *plod* all represent a very slow kind of movement, while for *trot, canter, gallop, lope, jog, run, dash,* and *scamper,* the movement is much more rapid. By listing *proud* vs. *not proud, short distance* vs. *long distance, goal oriented* vs. *non-goal oriented,* and *slow* vs. *fast* as feature dichotomies, we do not mean to imply that such distinctions are two-valent, i.e., all one or all the other. There are many expressions which are somewhere between *proud* and *not proud* between *short* and *long distance,* etc. Certainly *amble* or *saunter* is slower than *walk,* and *march* is faster than *walk.* And *jog* is slower than *run* which is slower than *dash.* In fact such expressions as *trot, canter, gallop,* and *lope,* although they are all fast, i.e., they are all within the speed range of *run,* are distinguished from each other on the basis of relative speed (although manner is also a consideration for this set).

All of the verbs of transportation which we have been considering have the same case frame. Since all such verbs represent movement from one place to another place, it is a requirement of this class of verbs that there be a Source, a Path, and a Goal in the deep structure.

Since a body in rest tends to stay in rest, there must be some activating force; it is therefore a further requirement of this class of verbs that there must be an Agent (more precisely, an Agent or a Force) in the deep structure. The basic case frame for verbs of transportation, therefore, is [————A S P G]. In addition, we noticed that there is often an Instrument associated with transportation verbs and that this Instrument is often incorporated into the verb rather than being stated as an object of a preposition. Let us therefore say that transportation verbs have the revised case frame [———— A S P G (I)]. There is still one other case that is appropriate, but not required, for verbs of transportation. This is the Object case. This Object may be stated as the direct object of the verb as in, "We brought *the children* with us." In fact, as was mentioned earlier, such expressions as *bring* and *take* are exactly equivalent to *come* and *go,* except that the former take an Object, i.e., they are transitive, while the latter do not take an Object, i.e., they are intransitive. As with intransitive verbs of transportation, it is often possible to incorporate the Instrument of transitive verbs of transportation as the following examples demonstrate, *boat, bus, canoe, cart, paddle, sail, ship, truck....* In fact, many of the words in this list can be either intransitive, as in, "We canoed from Lake Erie to Lake Michigan," or transitive, as in, "We canoed *the children* from Lake Erie to Lake Michigan." In view of these facts, we will again revise the case frame for transportation verbs to read as follows: [———— A S P G (I) (O)].

While verbs of transportation can be either transitive or intransitive, it is a requirement of verbs of transfer and of verbs of exchange that they be transitive. Verbs of transfer, in fact, have the same case frame as the transitive verbs of transportation. As examples, consider the following:

accept, acquire, borrow, bring, cast, catch, chuck, distribute, drop, export, fetch, give, grab, grant, grasp, hand, import, inherit, intercept, leave, lend, lift, lose, obtain, pilfer, pitch, present, publish, pull, push, receive, remove, rob, seize, send, shove, steal, throw, transfer, take, transmit, toss, will, win....

Just as it was logical for verbs of transportation to have *legs* as their most common Instrument, it is logical for verbs of transfer to have *arm* as their most common Instrument. This Instrument is often incorporated into the verb, either transparently as in *to hand* or opaquely as in *chuck, grab, intercept, pitch, seize, throw,* and *toss.*

There are several converses associated with verbs of this class such as *throw-catch, will-inherit, give-take, win-lose, lend-borrow, send-receive, buy-sell, pay-accept, rent to-rent from, (sub)let to-(sub)let from,* and *export-import.* However, discussion of such converses will be postponed until the chapter treating paraphrase.

Lexical features can be extracted out of verbs of transfer. For example, such expressions as *lend* and *borrow* are temporary, while *give* and *take* are permanent. *Rob, steal,* and *pilfer* are illegal, while *inherit, receive* and *transfer* are legal. *Seize* and *grab* indicate a fast action, while *acquire* and *inherit* indicate a slow action. *Distribute, publish, hand out,* and *pass out* can be used only for a large number of Objects, while *pass, pitch,* and *chuck* are usually used for a single Object. And finally, such words as *hand, hand off, seize, grab,* and *grasp* indicate a very close juxtaposition of the giver and the taker, while *throw, toss, pitch, cast, lateral,* and *chuck* indicate that the giver and taker are not close to each other.

Verbs of exchange can be thought of as verbs of double transfer. In a sentence like, "John acquired the house (from Mary) (for $15,000)," there are two Objects which change ownership. *The house* goes from Mary to John, and the *$15,000* goes from John to Mary. The case frame for verbs of exchange is [———— A O S G O S G]. For the person who believes that there must be a Path whenever there is a Source and a Goal, this case could be added twice to the case frame above. Verbs of exchange include the following:

acquire, buy, exchange, pay, receive, reimburse, rent, sell, spend, (sub)let, trade....

Such a verb as *acquire* can be either a verb of transfer or a verb of exchange depending on whether it represents a single or a double transfer of Objects.

As a final subcategory of verbs of motion, let us consider verbs of communication. Such verbs have the following case frame: [———— Agent, Experiencer, Object, Instrument]. At first glance, this case frame seems to differ greatly from that of other verbs of motion, but in fact it is very similar. Consider a sentence like, "John told Mary to do the dishes." In this sentence *John* is the Agent, *Mary* is the Experiencer, and *to do the dishes* is the abstract Object. But if viewed in a slightly different way, *John* is not only the Agent but the

Source as well; and *Mary* is not only the Experiencer but the Goal as well. This allows us to more clearly see the similarity between this case frame and that of other verbs of motion. But what is the Instrument in a sentence like, "John told Mary to do the dishes?" It is the vocal tract, and in fact, the vocal tract is the Instrument for most verbs of communication, including the following:

accuse, admit, apologize, ask, assert, blame, call, chatter, cite, comment, communicate, conclude, contend, cry, claim, deny, describe, divulge, drawl, enunciate, explain, forgive, holler, indicate, inform, imply, instruct, interrupt, maintain, mean, offer, point out, pray, promise, propose, prove, recite, refuse, remark, remind, reply, report, reveal, swear, talk, teach, tell, say, show, shout, sing, speak, sputter, stutter, suggest, vow, warn, whisper, whistle....

The nature of some verbs of this type is such that more than one Instrument is incorporated. For example, *demonstrate* and *show* include other parts of the human body as well as the voice, and *telephone* and *radio* include concrete Instruments as well as, or instead of, the human voice. In this latter type the Instrument is usually transparently incorporated, e.g., *cable, tape, telegraph, wire, radio, telephone....*

The vocal tract which is incorporated into the verbs above is necessarily a human vocal tract, for when an animal vocal tract is incorporated, it is usually the case that the incorporation opaquely indicates the kind of animal the sound is coming from as the following two colums suggest:

ANIMAL:	SOUND:
horse	whinney/neigh
cow	moo
lion/tiger/feline	growl/roar/purr
canine	bark/howl/bay
sheep	baa/bleat
turkey	gobble
pig	oink
goose	honk
duck	quack
chicken	cackle/cluck
rooster	crow/cock-a-doodle-doo
cat	meow/purr/hiss
dove/pigeon	coo

mouse	squeak
frog	croak
cricket	chirp
bird/chick	cheep/peep
crow	caw
snake	hiss
elephant	trumpet

In discussing one-place predicates we mentioned that there was a large class of verbs which represented instrumental sounds. A sentence like, "The steampipe hissed," was said to have the single-place case frame following: [———— I]. But now consider the sentence, "The snake hissed." Should this sentence not have been treated in the section on one-place predicates as having the case frame [———— A]? The answer is *no*. These animal sounds are truly verbs of communication. These are not random, accidental sounds but are intended to be heard either by a friend or a foe. These sounds indicate that the animal is afraid, or wants a mate, or is summoning its offspring, or that it is dangerous and must be avoided, or that there is an intruder in the area, etc. Since these animal sounds are verbs of communication, they have the case frame [———— A E O I] just like verbs of human communication.

VERBS OF LOCATION:

Verbs of location all have basically the same case frame. Verbs of containment, e.g., *to fill*, verbs of attachment, e.g., *to button*, verbs of enclosure, e.g., *to screen in*, and verbs of covering, e.g., *to asphalt*, all have an Agent, an Object, a Location, and an optional Instrument. The case frames of all four of these types of locative verbs would therefore be represented as [———— A O L (I)]. For all verbs of containment, the container itself is the Location or place into which the Object is put. In many instances this container is unspecified as for the following expressions:

empty, fill, keep, lay, load, overflow, place, post, pour, put, save, set, stack....

But more frequently, the Locative container is incorporated into the verb. It is by this process that a sentence like, "John put the groceries into a bag," becomes "John bagged the groceries." Verbs which are derived in approximately this manner include the following:

> board (up), bottle, box, bag, can, crate, coop (up), encase, encircle, fence, glass (in), house, package, pen (in), rope, sack, saucer, screen (in), shelve, table, tree, wall (in)....

There are a few problems with this category of verbs. *To box* as in, "The man boxed the oranges," is different from *to tree* as in, "The dog treed the cat." Although the Agent causes the Object to be in the container in both sentences, the Object itself has a much more active role in respect to the verb *to tree* than it has in respect to the verb *to box.* And a box is in fact a container, while a tree is not usually thought of as such. Nor are such things as *a circle, a saucer, a shelf, a table,* and perhaps even *a fence* and *a rope,* considered to be containers in the strict sense. It may be that this class of verbs is therefore really two classes—one with incorporated containers and one with incorporated surfaces.

It should be noticed that with verbs of containment the Object may be either entering the container, as in *fill* or *pour (in),* or leaving the container, as in *empty, pour out, overflow,* or *spill.* But whenever the Locative container is incorporated into the verb, as in *to bottle* or *to can,* then the Object must be entering rather than leaving the container. Not always, but very often, the Object for verbs of containment is a liquid. Another interesting fact is that sometimes it is not an actual container but rather the material out of which the container is made which becomes the verb, as in *to board (up), to glass (in), to screen (off),* etc.

Another class of locative verbs would be verbs of attachment, including the following:

> button, bolt, batten, cement, clamp, glue, mortar, nail, paste, pin, rivet, rope, screw, staple, string, tack, tape, wire....

All these words have the same case frame as verbs of containment, except that the Instrument is necessary to the case frame rather than optional: [---- A O L I]. It should be noticed that in all of the above verbs the Instrument is incorporated into the verb, so that *to button* means *to attach with a button, to clamp* means *to attach with a clamp,* etc. There are some verbs like this where the Instrument is not transparent. For example, *to sew* doesn't overtly tell that it is thread that is used, nor does *to stick* tell that it is glue which is used. Sometimes the Instrument is a material like *cement, glue, mortar,* or *paste,* but more often the Instrument is the type of thing thought of as an instrument or tool, e.g., *a nail, a rivet, a tack,* etc.

VERBS OF CONTACT:

There is a set of verbs which are half-way between verbs of location and verbs of contact. They have the same [−−−− A O L (I)] case frame. Examples include the following:

asphalt, butter, cement (over), dust (in the meaning of sprinkling on), fertilize, frost, grass, gravel, grease, hard top, oil, paint, polish, sod, sprinkle, sugar, varnish, (wall)paper, water (down), wax....

For each of these verbs, a sentence like, "The city covered the road with asphalt" can be converted into a sentence like, "The city asphalted the road." Although the Objects for such verbs are not incorporated, they very well could be, since each of these words occurs with an extremely limited range of Objects, as shown in the paired listing below:

VERB (WITH INSTRUMENT INCORPORATED):	OBJECT:
asphalt	road/parking lot
butter	bread/cracker
cement	driveway/sidewalk
dust	flowers/crop
fertilize	field
frost	cake
grass	yard/pasture
gravel	roadbed/yard
grease	machine
hardtop	roadbed
oil	machine
sugar	food (e.g., cereal)
varnish	furniture
(wall)paper	room
wax	floor

For some of these words, a specific Instrument is opaquely incorporated. *Butter,* for example, incorporates *knife, paint* and *varnish* incorporate *brush* or *roller,* and *sugar* incorporates *spoon* or *sprinkler.*

It is very interesting that verbs of contact have exactly the same case frame as the verbs of location we have just been considering: [———— A O L (I)], and in fact, it is probably best to think of verbs of location as a special subset of verbs of contact. For all verbs of location there is a kind of either "positive" or "negative" contact involved. Verbs of contact probably represent the largest single category of verbs. For this reason, the class of contact verbs is dividable into a large number of smaller classes. In addition to the locative verbs, which have already been discussed, there are verbs of primping or cleaning, verbs of carpentry, verbs of hunting, verbs of cultivation, verbs of sports and music, verbs of clothing, and many other subcategories of contact verbs. A few examples of each of these subcategories include the following:

PRIMPING OR CLEANING: brush, hose (down), iron, mop, paint, shave, sponge (off), sweep, vacuum....

CARPENTRY: chisel, drill, file, hammer, nail, plane, sand(paper), saw, screw, shovel, whittle, wrench....

HUNTING: chop, club, fire, net, pan, scalp, shoot, stab, trap....

SPORTS AND MUSIC: bat, check, fiddle, play, putt....

CLOTHING: bridle, cap, coat, dress, harness, hobble, saddle, shoe....

MISCELLANEOUS: lasso, rope, (paper)clip, Xerox, photograph, project, sail, slice, spoon, steer, (un)lock....

Since these words are all very specific, it is not surprising that they exhibit a great deal of lexical incorporation. Nearly all of the words above transparently incorporate an Instrument. For those that do not, there is normally an Instrument incorporated opaquely, as seen in the list below:

VERB:	OPAQUELY INCORPORATED INSTRUMENT:
shave	razor
sweep	broom
whittle	knife

chop	ax
fire	gun
scrape	tomahawk or knife
shoot	gun or bow
stab	knife
check	hockey stick
putt	golf club
lasso	lariat or rope
photograph	camera
project	projector
slice	knife
steer	steering wheel or rudder
(un)lock	key

The incorporation has to be opaque for *whittle, stab,* and *slice* because as a rule an Instrument can be incorporated transparently in only one word, and we have the verb *to knife* which is what a person might do to another person.

But the Instrument is not the only case which can be incorporated into verbs of contact. For example, *shave* incorporates the Object *face, sweep* incorporates the Object *floor, scalp* incorporates the Object *skin* and *hair, thresh* incorporates the Object *grain, bat* incorporates the Object *baseball* or *softball, play* incorporates the Object *music* or *sport, slice* incorporates the Object *food (or golfball)* and *(un)lock* incorporates the Object *lock.*

Some verbs of contact have developed metaphorical meanings; for example, we can *cap* a bottle and *coat* a wall with paint. And *to wrench* no longer bears a direct relationship with the actual wrench in a carpenter's tool case.

Contact verbs incorporating a part of the body include *feel, finger, pinch, pluck, touch, thumb,* and *(un)tie* which all incorporate finger or thumb; *sit* incorporates buttocks, *punt, kick,* and *boot* incorporate foot; *kneel* incorporates knees, and *crawl* incorporates hands and knees; *wave, embrace, hug,* and *grope* incorporate arm; *caress, clutch, grasp, handle, hold, grab,* and *milk* incorporate the whole hand; *paddle, pat, pet, slap, applaud, spank,* and *clap* incorporate only the flat of the hand, and *jab, punch, slug,* and *sock* incorporate the knuckles of the hand. Such words as *nurse* and *suckle* incorporate the breast of one person and the lips of the other. *Bite* incorporates the teeth, while *taste* and *lick* incorporate the tongue, and *kiss, sip,* and *suck* incorporate the lips. *Breathe* incorporates the nose or mouth, and *scan, read, stare at, eye, glance at, look at,* and *peruse* incorporate the eye. With these verbs incorporating eye, there is no actual contact except through light rays. Nevertheless we will put these verbs in the same general category as the true contact verbs since they share so many semantic and syntactic features. A somewhat broadened concept of *contact* will allow us to consider such verbs as *pass* and *miss* as contact verbs even though no actual contact is made.

VERBS OF EXPERIENCE:

We will now focus on the five body parts which are most used in perceiving the real world; these are the five senses: touch, taste, hearing, seeing, and smelling. For accuracy, a distinction needs to be made between verbs of contact and verbs of perception. This might be represented as follows, with note being made of the fact that the subject of a contact verb is an Agent, while the subject of a perception verb is an Experiencer.

BODY PART:	CONTACT VERB:	PERCEPTION VERB:
eye	look at	see
ear	listen to	hear
nose	sniff	smell
finger	touch	feel
tongue	lick	taste

It is probably true that the perception verbs *see, hear, smell, feel,* and *taste* all entail the contact verbs *look at, listen to, sniff, touch,* and *lick* or something of the sort, while the reverse is not necessarily true. A person can look at something without seeing it and can touch something without feeling it, etc. There is another set of verbs incorporating these same body parts, in which the Object is the subject of the sentence. When a person says, "The car looked perfect," "The band sounded great," "The coffee smelled good," "The material felt wonderful," and "the steak tasted good," he implies both the notion of contact and the notion of perception in the deep structure. For example, the sentence about the band implies both that someone listened to the band and that someone heard the band. A number of verbs of general perception are vague in indicating through which particular sense something is perceived, e.g., *learn, seem, feel, perceive*, etc.

In this analysis, we are putting verbs of experience into four subclasses. In addition to the verbs of sense which were just discussed, there are verbs of perception, verbs of psychological events, and verbs of possession. All four of these types of verbs of experience have Objects and an animate receiver of the Object which is the Experiencer, either literally or figuratively. Therefore verbs of experience can be thought of as having basically the same case frame: [———— E O].

Verbs of perception include the following:

assume, believe, calculate, comprehend, contemplate, consider, determine, discover, doubt, enlighten, entail, estimate, expect, experience, feel, find out, guess, hope, imagine, infer, know, learn, preclude, presuppose, presume, reckon, regret, remember, resolve, sense, solve, suppose, suspect, think, understand, forget, wonder....

Verbs of psychological events are very similar to the verbs of perception, except that for verbs of perception, the Object is merely perceived in some way, while for verbs of psychological events, there is some sort of positive or negative reaction on the part of the Experiencer. Verbs of psychological events include the following:

adore, amaze, amuse, anger, annoy, appal, appeal to, appreciate, arouse, bore, bother, delight, desire, discourage, disappoint, disgust, disturb, embarrass, enjoy, entertain, excite, fear, frighten, grieve, hate, interest, irritate, like, please, puzzle, relieve, sadden, satisfy, scare, shock, stun, startle, surprise, thrill, tickle, tire, want, weaken, worry....

Some words which are psychological in nature are very closely associated with sex. Such words include *arouse, excite, thrill, tease, seduce,* and *rape.* These words require an Agent, so we might list a case frame for this subset of psychological events as [———— A E O]. Notice that these verbs are much more active in nature than are the other verbs of psychological events. It is possible, but not necessary, with nearly all verbs of psychological events to have an Agent. For example, the sentence, "John frightened the baby," is ambiguous in a way that the sentence, "The darkness frightened the baby" is not. In the first sentence, *John* could have frightened the baby intentionally, in which case *John* is the Agent as well as the Object. However, in the second sentence, *the darkness* could not possibly be an Agent because it is inanimate and therefore could not act intentionally. To accomodate these situations, perhaps it would be best to include in the case frame an optional Agent [———— (A) E O].

Since verbs of psychological events contain some positive or negative reaction on the part of the Experiencer, they can easily be paired off according to whether this reaction is positive or negative, as follows:

NEGATIVE REACTION:	POSITIVE REACTION:
appall	delight
anger	please
annoy	please/entertain
bother	relieve/let alone
discourage	encourage
disappoint	please/interest/delight
disgust	amuse/arouse/relieve/excite
dislike	appeal to/appreciate/like
disturb	calm
embarrass	set at ease
fear/frighten/scare	relieve
grieve	hearten
hate/abhor	adore/love/desire
irritate	please/let alone
shock/stun/startle	amaze/surprise/thrill
tire/weaken	strengthen
worry	relieve

In addition to the negative-positive distinction noted above, there are other semantic features which can be extracted from verbs of psychological events. For example, *startle, surprise, shock,* and *stun* represent a fast action, while *annoy, bother, appeal to,* and *please* have no indication of speed.

Since verbs of ownership are two-place predicates with an Experiencer and an Object, they are also classed in the very broad category of verbs of Experience. Such verbs as *belong, have, hold, lack, need, own, possess, require,* and *want* are verbs of ownership. It will be immediately noticed that some of these verbs indicate ownership, while others indicate the lack of ownership. Such verbs as *belong, have, hold, own,* and *possess* fall into the first category, while *lack, need, require,* and *want* fall into the second category. In addition, such words as *belong, own,* and *possess* indicate a more permanent, more legal type of ownership than do *have* or *hold.* Verbs of transfer, whether they are permanent (*give, take*) or temporary (*lend, borrow*); legal (*inherit, will, donate, transfer, receive*) or illegal (*rob, steal, pilfer, shoplift*); or any other category, result in a type of ownership. For example, if we say, "John inherited $100," we are implying that he has it or at least that he had it for a while. It might be argued that calling *John* the Experiencer in both "John enjoyed the movie" and in "John has $100" is a kind of equivocation. This is a problem not yet solved.

VERBS OF CHANGE:

All verbs of change must have an Object associated with them, and this Object must have a state, which we will call Source. This Source is initially different from the final state, which we will call Goal. The change which takes place between Source and Goal must be caused by something, either an Agent or a Force. Usually it is an Agent, and the Agent uses an Instrument, possibly a body part, to bring about the change. We will say then, that verbs of change must have the following case frame: [---- A (I) O G]. However, we'll discover later that when a person or animal is changed rather than an object, the case frame is slightly different: instead of having an Object, it has an Experiencer and reads [---- A (I) E S G].

In addition to the distinction between whether the thing changed is an object (Object) or an animal (Experiencer), there are two additional dimensions. On one hand, the change can be either creative, destructive, or merely a neutral alteration; on the other hand, the change can be partial as in *puncture* or total as in *demolish.* We will begin by discussing verbs which merely indicate an alteration of an object. There are certain verbal affixes which indicate change. One of these is *en* which can be either a prefix or a suffix, or even both as in *enliven.* Examples of verbs of change which have this *en* in them include:

blacken, brighten, broaden, darken, deaden, deafen, encourage, enlighten, enliven, enslave, fasten, fatten, freshen, flatten, frighten, gladden, harden, heighten, lengthen, lighten, madden, moisten, redden, roughen, sharpen, shorten, sicken, soften, straighten, strengthen, sweeten, thicken, whiten, worsen....

Another affix which indicates a change of state is the suffix -*ize* as in the following expressions:

anglicize, capitalize, civilize, colonize, deputize, dramatize, familiarize, idolize, immortalize, immunize, individualize, ionize, legalize, localize, maximize, mechanize, minimize, mobilize, modernize, naturalize, neutralize, oxidize, personalize, pluralize, popularize, rationalize, stabilize, standardize, sterilize, tranquilize, vaporize, victimize, vitalize, vulcanize, westernize....

And still another affix which indicates a change of state is the suffix -*ify* as in the following expressions:

beautify, clarify, codify, deify, glorify, liquify, mummify, personify, purify, qualify, simplify, specify, unify....

But while many change-of-state expressions are marked with distinct suffixes, many are not. The following expressions represent changes of state even though there is no overt suffix:

bleach, break, enthuse, fade, freeze, heat, kill, lay, learn, melt, place, put, raise, remind, rot, scald, set, show, teach, tell....

All of the examples of change-of-state verbs discussed so far have required an Agent. In many cases the only difference between two change-of-state verbs is that one requires an Agent, i.e., is causative, while the other does not. Consider the following pairs of change-of-state verbs:

AGENT REQUIRED:	AGENT NOT REQUIRED:	RESULTANT STATE:
teach	learn	educated
kill	die	dead
raise	rise	risen
set	sit	set
lay/place/put	lie	lying
forgive	apologize	forgiven
remind	remember	awareness
show	see	knowing
tell	hear	knowing

But more often the same form is used either causatively (with an Agent), or non-causatively (without an Agent). On the surface, the causatives can be distinguished from the non-causatives by the fact that the former are transitive while the latter are intransitive. The following words can be used in this way either with or without an Agent:

blacken, brighten, darken, redden, shorten, whiten, heat, rot, fade, break, freeze, melt, liquify, evaporate....

ϡ is only a beginning to this list. It could be extended for many pages because the normal situation in English is to use the same verb either transitively or intransitively.

Although there are a number of change-of-state verbs such as *adapt, alter, bend, change, fold,* and *repair* which do not seem to logically incorporate anything except possibly *manner,* lexical incorporation is a common phenomenon for verbs of change. Since most of this incorporation is opaque rather than transparent, these words are presented in the following pairings, matching the verb with the incorporated Instrument:

CHANGE-OF-STATE VERB:	INCORPORATED MATERIAL (INSTRUMENT):
dampen	water
douse	water
dye	dye
electrify	electricity
fade	light
flood	water
freeze	cold
ice	cold
light	light
pepper	pepper
salt	salt
season	seasoning
shock	electricity
spice (up)	spice
turn off	fluid or electricity
turn on	fluid or electricity
wash	water
wet (down)	water

To this point we have been considering verbs which indicate a slight alteration of the item being affected. Although the item is different in some respect(s) before and after the change of state, it is still basically the same item before and after the alteration. In the other two classes of change-of-state verbs, the item either does not exist before the change of state, i.e., the item is created, or the item does not exist after the change of state, i.e., the item is destroyed. These two categories can be labeled verbs of creation and verbs of destruction respectively. All verbs of change, whether they are verbs of alteration, verbs of creation, or verbs of destruction have the same case frame: [———— A (I) O S G]. The difference between these three sub-classes can be explained totally in terms of the difference in the nature of the Source and the Goal. For verbs of alteration, the Source and the Goal are basically the same. For verbs of creation, the Source is random bits of material, and the Goal is these same bits of material after they have been put together in some meaningful way. For verbs of destruction, the Source is the completed item, and the Goal is the random bits of material. In one sense, verbs of creation are more basic than verbs of destruction because something cannot be destroyed unless it has first been created, and as a result, exists. The following words are verbs of creation:

> assemble, beat, blend, build, compose, create, design, develop, erect, form, grow, letter, make, mix, paint, pencil in, shape, stir, whip, write....

One of the semantic areas which is particularly loaded with verbs of creation is the area of cooking. This can be seen in the above list by observing such expressions as *beat, blend, mix, stir* and *whip.* There are also a number of more specific words which lexically incorporate both the Instrument heat and the Object food:

> bake, boil, broil, brown, cook, crisp, fry, heat, roast, toast, simmer, sizzle, stew....

Verbs of destruction differ from each other in a number of ways. The thing destroyed can be either inanimate (Object) or animate (Experiencer). The destruction can be total or partial. Various deep cases can be lexically incorporated into the verb. And finally, each word differs from other words in the manner in which the destruction is carried out. In the discussion below, all but the last of these four distinctions will be investigated. Let us first consider partial inanimate destruction in which the Instrument is not incorporated: words belonging to this class would include the following:

core, carve, crack, cut, disarm, divide, fade, gash, lacerate, peel, pit, puncture, rip, scrape, seed, shake, slash, slice, snap, spill, stir, string, tear, unarm....

The words *seed, string,* and *disarm* have as Objects *clouds, beans,* and *weapon* respectively. For *seed* and *string* the Object is not deletable, probably because these are not common meanings for these particular words, but for *disarm* the intended meaning is still clear when the Object is deleted. There are some partial inanimate destruction verbs which incorporate an Instrument. In fact, a common device in English is to change a sentence like, "John (partially) eradicated the message with a pencil," into a sentence like, "John pencilled out the message." Notice that by this process, the Instrument is transparently incorporated into the verb, and the word *out* is added. Other examples which illustrate this process include *chalk out, crayon out, ink out, paint out, x out,* etc.

There are also words which indicate the total destruction of an inanimate Object. These include the following:

blow up, bomb, break, burn (up or down), crush, demolish, destroy, dissolve, dynamite, eradicate, erase, melt, mutilate, obliterate, raze, ruin, shatter, smash, strafe, tear (up or down)....

There are also verbs indicating partial animate destruction. These include the following:

assault, attack, blind, conquer, defeat, dehorn, dismember, elbow, exile, impale, gun down, hurt, lacerate, ravage, shoot, shoulder, stab, stone, vanquish, wound....

It should be noticed that some of these verbs are stronger than others. *To elbow* or *to shoulder* someone is not nearly as strong or as permanent as *to blind* or *to shoot* that same person. The verb *dismember* indicates that the animal (usually a human) is not totally destroyed. Syntactically it would be reasonable to assume that *behead* or *decapitate* would be examples of *dismemberment,* but semantically they are not, since *dismember* implies that the amputated limb is something other than the head. Other words which might be on the borderline between total and partial destruction are *impale* or *stone* since these could result in death. Verbs which are clearly total animate destruction include the following:

annihilate, assassinate, behead, decapitate, electrocute, exterminate, gas, hang, kill, murder, martyr, quarter....

It is interesting how these words are distinguished from each other. Of these eleven words, the word *kill* is the most general. It includes all the other words and it could be used in any place that one of them would appear. Because it is so general, it has the fewest number of specific semantic features. The other words have the same semantic features as *kill*, but in addition they have more specific features. *Kill*, and therefore the other words in this class, can be lexically decomposed into the more primitive elements "cause to become dead." All of the words of this set, indicate a change of state (and therefore must have an Object or an Experiencer in their case frame), and since the change of state from alive to dead is one which is applicable in the literal sense only to animate beings, this means that only Experiencers (not Objects) are appropriate in the case frame. And since all these words indicate cause there must be an Agent present, and Agents use Instruments, so an Instrument is also appropriate to the case frame. Some of the specific ways in which these basically similar words differ from each other include the fact that *annihilate* refers to the killing of a large number of people, while *exterminate* refers to the killing of a large number of animals or humans considered as animals. *Behead* and *decapitate* indicate what part of the body is removed to produce the change of state from alive to dead. *Electrocute, gas, hang,* and perhaps *quarter* indicate the material or the instrument used to cause the death. *Murder* indicates the illegality of the action and *martyr* and *assassinate* indicate to some extent the reason for the killing, and/or the importance of the person who was killed.

VERBS OF CONTROL:

It is the Agent case which has the most control over the other cases. It was mentioned before that Agents control Instruments and that Instruments in turn have an effect on Objects. Consider a sentence like, "The president appointed John." The verb in this sentence seems to be a two-place predicate co-occurring with an Agent (the President) and an Experiencer (John). But in fact, this sentence is incomplete. It is true that *John* is an Experiencer in relation to the verb *appoint,* but in some sense, *John* is also an Agent. When a person uses the sentence, "The President appointed John," he is stating explicitly that the President did something, i.e., *appoint John,* but he is also stating implicitly that John will do something, i.e., fill a particular role. A paraphrase of the sentence could be, "The President appointed John to do something." This dual role is characteristic of verbs of control. They have an Agent, and they have an Experiencer. In addition, they have an embedded action sometimes in the form of an embedded sentence. In this embedded sentence, the Experiencer of the main sentence now acts as the Agent. This is either stated explicitly or implied, depending on the particular verb of control. The main feature which distinguishes the different sub-classes of verbs of control from each other would be strength. A weak verb of control would be *allow,* a stronger verb of control would be *encourage,* and a still stronger verb of control would be *force.*

Verbs of allowance include the following:

> allow, appoint, authorize, call on, challenge, choose, commission, constrain, dare, engage, elect, employ, empower, enable, entitle, hire, let, name, nominate, permit, privilege, tell, write, license, permit....

Verbs of aid are like verbs of allowance except the Agent of the main sentence not only has control over the secondary action, but is actually an Agent in helping to carry out the secondary action. Such verbs include the following:

> aid, assist, coach, design, help, lead, prepare, remind, teach, train, demonstrate, show....

Now consider verbs of encouragement, such as the following:

> admonish, advise, arouse, appeal to, ask, beg, beseech, caution, communicate, condemn, counsel, direct, encourage, enjoin, entreat, exhort, fire up, goad, induce, inspire, instruct, invite, persuade, lead, prompt, provoke, request, say to, stimulate, stir, tempt, urge, warn....

Verbs of expectation are stronger than verbs of allowance, aid, or encouragement. They include the following:

> count on, desire, expect, intend, (would) like, look for, mean for, oblige, prefer, seek for, trust, want....

They imply that the secondary Agent has some sort of an obligation to the primary Agent to accomplish the action of the embedded sentence. Finally, the strongest control verbs of all are those of force. They include the following:

> assign, cause, coerce, command, compel, consign, forbid, force, get, incite, make, order, require, prevail upon....

SYMMETRICAL PREDICATES:

One type of symmetrical predicate is that which has two Objects in its case frame and no other cases. These predicates represent states rather than actions, and in fact they compare the state of one of the Objects to the state of the other. These include such expressions as *equivalent, same, similar, be like, appear like, resemble, identical, equal,* and the various sense verbs combined with *like* such as *feel like, smell like, sound like, look like,* and *taste like.* The reason that these are called symmetrical predicates is that the two Objects can be reversed without affecting the meaning of the sentence. Thus, if "A is similar to B," then it is necessarily true that "B is similar to A." When the word *touch* represents a state rather than an action, it is also a symmetrical predicate, for "A is touching B" if and only if "B is touching A." From the examples given so far, it would appear that symmetrical predicates always indicate a resemblance between two Objects. This is not always the situation, since such expressions as *different, differ, distinct,* and *contrast* are also symmetrical because "A is different from B" if and only if "B is different from A." It is also possible to have two Agents in a single case frame. There is a sense in which an expression like *marry* or *kiss* or *collide with* are also symmetrical predicates. John can marry Alice if and only if Alice marries John as part of the same ceremony. Therefore, saying that John married Alice is equivalent to saying that Alice married John. It is not the case, however, that saying that the preacher married John and Alice is equivalent to saying that John and Alice married the preacher. The expression *kiss* is ambiguous as to whether or not it is symmetrical. Sometimes when a person says, "John kissed Mary," he means, "John and Mary kissed each other," but it is entirely possible for John to kiss Mary without Mary kissing John. Finally, if car A collides with car B, which is moving, it is also true that car B collides with car A. But on the other hand, if car A collides with a tree, it is not true that a tree collides with car A. Such words as *discuss, negotiate, fight,* and *interact,* as well as *gather, assemble, pair off,* and even *numerous* are additional examples of symmetrical predicates.

SET CASE FRAMES:

Symmetrical predicates must necessarily be two-place predicates. Furthermore, both of these cases must be the same. In "John resembles Harry," both *John* and *Harry* are Objects. In "The Cadillac collided with the Jaguar," both *the Cadillac* and *the Jaguar* are Instruments. Symmetrical predicates are unique in a number of ways. Either two noun phrases can be reversed for such predicates, or they can become pluralized, so that "John resembles Harry" can become "Harry resembles John," or "They resemble each other," or "The Cadillac collided with the Jaguar" can become simply, "They collided." The point is that some verbs require a set (larger than one) of cases rather than a single occurence of a case for their case frame. This is true not only of the symmetrical predicates mentioned above, but also of such expressions as *co-author, cooperate,* and *costar,* which require more than a single Agent, and also of *distribute, publish, hand out,* and *pass out,* which require more than a single Object.

CONCLUSION:

Most semanticists have felt that it is necessary to have a syntactic justification for semantic categories. For example, they separated such stative verbs as *believe, know, regret, expect, hope, have, resemble, cost, want, lack,* and *like* from such active verbs as *persuade, force, listen, watch, order, make, swim,* and *sit.* Some of their justification for this was the fact that active verbs can become cleft sentences, e.g., "What he did was persuade me to come," while stative verbs can not, e.g., *"What he did was believe that I came." Also, active verbs can become imperatives, e.g., "Persuade him to come!" but stative verbs can not *"Believe that he came!" Active verbs can accept manner adverbials, e.g., "He painstakingly persuaded me to come," but stative verbs cannot, e.g., *"He painstakingly believed that I came." Active verbs can accept the negative of permission, e.g., "He may not persuade me to come" but stative verbs cannot, e.g., *"He may not believe that I came." Active verbs can be made progressive, e.g., "He is persuading me to come," but the stative verbs cannot, e.g., *"He is believing that I came." Active verbs can be pronominalized by *do so,* e.g., "John persuaded me to come, but Mary didn't do so," but stative verbs can not, e.g., *"John believed that I came, but Mary didn't do so." In addition, active verbs can take such things as locative expressions, benefactive expressions, and instrumental expressions, while stative verbs can not. Such observations are important, but they are mainly observations about the surface structure. In this chapter we have attempted to show how introspective, intuitive judgments can be used to equate semantic categories with case frames of predicates. There was a general absence of syntactic evidence throughout the chapter. The semantic categories and the case frames that we have postulated are not of the nature that they should be justified by syntactic evidence. They are basic, deep structure facts. We are not saying that there is no relationship between semantics and syntax; indeed there is a very high correlation between the two. We are merely saying that semantics should be studied in its own right, and that in general, it is the semantics that is placing the constraints on the syntax rather than the other way about.

VIII. Antonymy

As shown in Chapter III, understanding homonyms (either homophones or homographs) and heteronyms presents little difficulty because there is only a single semantic constraint involved in the definition. This constraint is that the words, although having the same spelling or pronunciation, have a different set of semantic features. The extent and the nature of the difference is totally irrelevant. But this is not true of antonyms, because it is not enough to say that antonyms have different phonological structures, different orthographies, and different meanings. There are many words which could fit this definition but still not be antonyms. If we changed the expression *different meanings* to *opposite meanings* we may be closer to a precise definition, but there are significant problems even with this revised definition.

For example, let us consider the antonyms *black* and *white*. In some sense these two words are opposite in meaning, yet to a very large extent they are similar in meaning. They are both qualities (adjectives); and they are both color words and therefore have basically the same syntactic distribution. They differ mainly in that *black* means absence of color while *white* means total color. But even people who are not aware of this physical difference consider these two words to be perceptual antonyms. Now, what is the antonym of *red*? A person who knows about a color spectrum might say that its antonym is *purple* since red and purple come at opposite ends of the spectrum. But someone familiar with a color wheel might say *green* is the antonym of red since it is directly across from it. An interior decorator who thinks about color in appropriate color groupings or in relationship to its psychological effect on people might give a different antonym, and a lay person would probably be hard pressed to think of any antonym at all. But certainly he would not say *car* or *walk*, although *red* is more different from *car* or *walk* than it is from *green* or *purple*.

Now consider two other words. What are the antonyms of *always* and *hot*? Probably without hesitation, a person would say that the antonym of *always* is *never* and the antonym of *hot* is *cold*. In words like this where continuums are clearly evident, then it is easy to pick out the polar extremes as opposites or antonyms. Something toward—but not clear to—the end of the continuum like *warm* would have as its antonym something toward—but not clear to—the other end of the continuum like *cool*. But this becomes more complicated. What is the antonym of *seldom*? Is it *often, usually,* or *frequently?* The point is that in subjective continuums where there are many contrasted terms, antonyms are indistinct. In a sense *often, usually,* and *frequently* are all antonyms of *seldom,* and also of *rarely, infrequently,* and *once in a while.*

As a beginning point, let us assume that antonyms are words which have the same strict subcategorization requirements and the same selection restrictions, but whose most specific semantic features are polar extremes of each other. For example, *shout* and *whisper* are both verbs of communication which take human subjects. They must have a direct object, which is the communication itself, as in "John shouted/whispered 'Come here!' " We can see that *shout* and *whisper* are similar to each other in a number of respects, and also that they are similar in the same ways to the words *say* and *yell*. How is it, then, that we know that *shout* and *whisper* are antonyms and that *shout* and *say* are not antonyms? Furthermore, how do we know that *yell* and *shout* are not antonyms, and in fact that *whisper* is as much an antonym for *yell* as it is for *shout?* These facts can only be understood by comparing these words with each other on a scale of loudness. When this is done, the following system emerges:

whisper		shout
		yell

SOFT	LOUD

In other words, *whisper* is an antonym of either *shout* or *yell* according to the feature *loudness*. In fact, we can say that the four words *whisper, sigh, murmur,* and *mumble* are antonyms of the five words *holler, shout, yell, call,* and *cry* on the basis of loudness. To be exact antonyms, the words must differ from each other *only* by the feature of loudness. In other words, they must represent the same level of formality, the same negative or positive connotations, the same social register, etc., but since these are very difficult things to measure, we will oversimplify by saying that any one of the "loud words" could be correctly given as an antonym of any one of the "soft words." But certainly loudness is not the only basis of antonymy. Indeed there are a great many other semantic continuums which may also be used.

In analyzing antonymy, it is important to realize that only one semantic continuum at a time can be used in setting up opposites. For example, in the real world the end result whether someone *shouts* or *whispers,* is that something is communicated. So on this basis, the two words are synonyms, not antonyms. Instead something like *remained silent* would be the antonym for both *shout* and *whisper.* Another feature which verbs of communication might be ranked on is strength or definiteness with which something is said. With this feature in mind, *vow* and *swear to* are antonyms of such expressions as *hint at* and *imply.* But if the feature being contrasted is speed, then *chatter* and *drawl* are antonyms. But if the important feature is distinctness, then *enunciate* is the antonym of both *chatter* and *drawl.*

Verbs of movement can be ranked according to the feature of strength. For example, *prance, strut, goosestep,* and *promenade* are all at the strong energetic end of the scale, while at the weak or tired end of the scale would be *limp, stagger, falter along,* and *plod.* Another feature that might be used to identify antonyms in these and similar verbs would be whether or not they are goal oriented. For example, a person *stalks, jumps,* or *dashes* only with a particular goal in mind. But in contrast when there is no goal, he *meanders, wanders,* or *saunters.* These same words could be contrasted according to speed where an antonym for *dash* might be *creep* or *crawl.* Or according to manner, an antonym for *saunter* might be *march.* It is the linguistic context in which words appear that focuses attention on particular features to be contrasted. This context becomes very important with words which have multiple sets of semantic features. For example if people are talking about age and someone says the word *man* then the contrasting pair is apt to be *men* and *boys.* But if the conversation is about the conflict between the sexes, then the antonymous pair will be *men* and *women.* And if the conversation is about humanity in general then the contrasting pair will be *man* and *animal.* It is interesting that *women* who are specifically excluded from the middle usage of *man* are included in the latter usage. The confusion which sometimes surrounds this word is a result of not knowing which semantic feature is intended as the basis for contrast.

A very common basis for distinguishing antonyms is to evaluate them as *good* or *bad.* Sometimes this evaluation is objective, but more often it is extremely subjective and open to individual interpretation. And such concepts as *good* and *bad* are so general that they seem to have little meaning unless they are further broken down. One *good-bad* distinction which can be made is between legal and illegal activities. For example *to purchase* something is legal, but *to shoplift* something is illegal. *To inherit* something is legal, but *to steal* something is illegal. This means then that on the *good-bad* feature these words are antonyms of each other. Other words which are probably considered antonyms on a more general positive vs. negative scale include the following:

POSITIVE:	NEGATIVE:
comfort	frighten
please	anger/annoy
encourage	discourage
amuse	disgust
calm	disturb
adore/love	abhor/hate
amaze/surprise/thrill	shock/stun
happy/contented	sad/despondent
fortunate	unfortunate

grateful	ungrateful
intelligent/smart	stupid/dumb
popular	unpopular
discrete	indiscrete
wise	foolish/silly
fair/impartial	unfair/prejudiced
pleasant	unpleasant/irritating
useful	useless

A distinction which needs to be mentioned is that there are different levels of antonymy, i.e., that between a positive action, a zero action, and a negative action. For example one antonym of *helpful* is *helpless,* which indicates a zero action. But another antonym is *troublesome* which represents an action achieving the opposite effect from a *helpful* action. This same process can be seen in such sentences as, "John told the truth, but Mary didn't say a word" vs. "John told the truth, but Mary told a lie," and "John always has good luck, but nothing ever happens to Mary" vs. "John always has good luck, but Mary always has bad luck." Although these sentences have phrasal rather than word antonymy, the process is the same as with the words in the following lists which illustrate the three-way kind of antonymy which we are talking about. The words in the right and left columns can be used as general antonyms of each other while under certain circumstances the words in the middle column can also be used as antonyms of either the right or left-column words.

ACTION OR STATE:	ZERO ACTION:	OPPOSITE ACTION:
make	do nothing	destroy
accept	ignore	refuse
persuade	say nothing	dissuade
approve of	ignore	censure
force	let	forbid

Practically all verbs showing an action and an opposite action could be listed on a three-place scale with the middle place being filled by something like *do nothing.* For example this zero action column could go between the following two lists showing an action and an opposite action:

ACTION:	OPPOSITE ACTION:
freeze	melt
condense	evaporate
liquefy	solidify
liquefy	evaporate
tie	untie
wash	dirty
turn on	turn off
make	demolish
form	dissolve
write	erase
hire	fire
dress	undress
harness	unharness
bridle	unbridle
saddle	unsaddle

Nearly all verbs of creation can be contrasted with verbs of destruction as actions and opposite actions. In determining whether a certain action is opposite another action, not only the actions but the resultant states must be considered. Each of the above actions results in a state which will allow the opposite action to take place. For example if we freeze something then it can be melted, then it can be frozen again and then melted again. Theoretically this circular process can go on forever. The same is true with *wash* vs. *dirty* and *tie* vs. *untie,* etc. Antonyms based on an action vs. an opposite action are circular. The application of one of these words sets up the condition or state required for the application of the other word. And in fact, the same concept cannot be applied more than once unless its opposite is applied alternately. For example you can not *unharness* a horse unless it has been *harnessed*, and it doesn't make sense that someone would try to *harness* a horse that was already harnessed.

One of the words in the above list, *sublimate,* seems to be deviant because it has no opposite word. The concept exists, but English does not happen to have a common individual word to express it. The word *sublimate* means to change from a solid to a gas without becoming a liquid. The opposite of this would be to change from a gas to a solid without becoming a liquid as when frost forms from moisture in the air. When this occurs, whether or not there is a specific term for it, then the situation is back to the state where *sublimation* can occur again, so the cycle has been restored.

A different problem occurs with the word *liquefy*. This word has the opposite problem of *sublimate*, in that it has too many rather than not enough antonyms. Both *solidify* and *evaporate* are antonyms of *liquefy*, as can be seen in the following diagram:

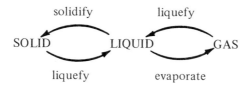

The meaning of *liquefy* is "to change into a liquid." There are two different things that can happen to a liquid. It can evaporate (become a gas), or it can solidify (become a solid). This means that the term *liquefy* is part of two different but related cycles. This is one small illustration of the way that real-world circumstances must be taken into account when analyzing antonymy.

The last concept which we will mention under antonymy is one that will be treated more fully in the next chapter on paraphrase. It is the difference between converse pairs of words like *lend* and *borrow, throw* and *catch, teach* and *learn*, etc. These are pairs of words which refer to the same real-world event. The feature on which they are antonymous is point of view, i.e., is the action being viewed through the eyes of the donor or the receiver? But as far as communicating what took place, they tell about the same situation and will therefore be talked about in the next chapter.

IX. Synonymy and Paraphrase

It is impossible for any sentence in one language to have exactly the same meaning as any sentence in another language. It is also impossible for any sentence in a particular language to have exactly the same meaning as any other sentence in that same language. If no two sentences mean exactly the same thing, then how is it possible to talk about synonymy and paraphrase at all?

It is possible because such concepts as *synonymy* and *paraphrase* are used in two different senses. Consider the two sentences, "John Jones is a police officer," as compared with, "My next door neighbor is a pig." In one sense these two sentences are synonymous with (i.e., they are paraphrases of) each other, but in another important sense they are not. If both of these sentences refer to the same real-life facts, i.e., John Jones is my neighbor and he is a policeman, then they can be said to be paraphrases of each other because they have the same truth value. If the first sentence is true, so is the second sentence; if the first is false, the second is also false. To say one of these sentences is to imply the existence of the other. Person A in a family might use the first sentence, and Person B in the same family might use the second sentence to refer to exactly the same real-life situation. Or Person A might use each of the sentences at a different time, depending on how he happened to be feeling.

This loose meaning of paraphrase, which refers to the denotative relationship between a sentence and the real world, is the definition which will be used throughout this chapter. It must be cautioned, however, that such sentences are not paraphrases in the precise sense. The difference between "John Jones is a police officer," and "My next door neighbor is a pig," are numerous. The first, but not the second, implies that the listener already knows what person is being referred to with the name *John Jones.* And it implies that the speaker has a respect for the law, and/or that the listener has a respect for the law. The second sentence, but not the first, implies that the policeman himself may not be of the highest character. It also may imply that the speaker does not feel good about his neighborhood. There are many other differences of implication and connotation between these two sentences, although they refer to the same real-world fact.

For our present purposes, then, synonymy and paraphrase will refer only to the truth value of particular sentences. Even though two sentences differ from each other in such things as connotations, level of formality, assumed knowledge of the listeners, knowledge and intentions of the speaker, and focus or topicalization of various lexical items, the sentences may still be considered synonymous if they relate the same denotative information about the real world.

There are two kinds of synonymy. One kind is transformational, which results from grammatical changes in the sentence. The other kind is lexical, which results from a use of different words. Transformational synonymy can be further divided into three types of operations: permutation, reduction, and deletion. In general, these three types of transformations do not affect the meaning of the sentence as a whole. Permutation or inversion transformations change the order of the various words in a sentence with respect to each other. The result is not a change in meaning, but rather a change in emphasis. Typically these permutation transformations are called topicalization transformations because they change the focus (or topic), or change the distribution of old and new information (topic and comment). It should be noticed that both reduction and deletion transformations are typically possible if, and only if, the reduced or deleted stretch has been stated previously. This is why pronouns (and pro-adverbs, pro-verbs, pro-sentences, etc.) have antecedents, and this is why there are so many occurrences of equi-NP deletion in languages. This is the kind of deletion which takes place when the subject would be repeated as in "John wanted Mary to go," compared to *"John wanted John to go." In this latter sentence the second *John* must be deleted since it is a repeat of the subject, and the result is, "John wanted to go."

Because of the semantic constraint that words are not generally reduced or deleted unless there is an antecedent, only material that has been stated previously and is therefore semantically redundant is reduced or deleted. Hence semantic information is usually not lost. And even when some semantic information is lost, the reduced sentence is still a paraphrase of the fuller sentence. It has simply become more vague. This vagueness does not violate our notion of paraphrase since this merely implies a different amount of prior knowledge on the part of the listener, or else a different intent of communication on the part of the speaker.

The three types of lexical paraphrase can be described as synonyms, converses, and lexical incorporations. We can say that the sentences, "I saw a policeman," and "I saw a cop," are paraphrases of each other because the only difference between the two sentences is the substitution of the word *cop* for *policeman* and these two words are synonyms. Again, the two sentences refer to the same incident in real life. But now consider a sentence like, "John sold a typewriter to me for $50.00," as compared to "I bought a typewriter from John for $50.00." Although these two sentences look very different from each other on the surface, they in fact refer to the same real-world event. In fact, we can say that "John sold a typewriter to me for $50.00," is true if and only if "I bought a typewriter from John for $50.00" is true. That is, these two sentences have exactly the same truth value; they refer to the same real-world event. Verbs like *buy* and *sell*—which have the same real-world elements associated with them, but which arrange these elements differently as subjects and objects, and which use prepositions differently, but which refer to the same real-world event—are called converses. Again, since our notion of paraphrase is based on the relationship between the linguistic form, and the real-world meaning, sentences containing converses are said to be paraphrases of each other.

Lexical incorporation occurs when two verbs such as *cause* and *die* are combined with the adverb *illegally* to form the single lexical item *murder*. Another example of this process is when the verb *put* is combined with the prepositional phrase *in a box* to form the single verb *to box*. Lexical incorporation is an extremely common process in any language, and it is through this process that languages develop efficiency. For example, all the information incorporated in, "the animal which has wool, and bleats, and has hooves, and whose babies are called lambs, and which is a domestic quadruped which lives on farms and which travels in flocks," is changed to the single lexical item *sheep*.

What has been suggested so far is that paraphrase can be outlined as follows:

I. Transformational
A. Permutations
B. Reductions
C. Deletions
II. Lexical
A. Synonyms
B. Converses
C. Lexical Incorporations

We will now look at each of these types of paraphrase in more detail.

TRANSFORMATIONAL PARAPHRASE:

Permutation transformations are also called inversion or movement transformations. The nature of such transformations is that some word or group of words is changed from one place in a sentence to another place. Typically such transformations do not change or delete meanings, but they usually change the focus or the formality or the style or the commonness of the sentence. Because movement transformations affect the focus and may even change the distribution of old and new information, they are called topicalization transformations. In some languages the word order is very free, and for these languages, there are a great many different orders of constituents which might be paraphrases of each other. Even in such a language as English, however, where the word order is quite fixed, there are still many different constituent orders which are paraphrases.

Let us begin by discussing adverb movement. A sentence like, "John slowly entered the room," means the same as "Slowly John entered the room," or "John entered the room slowly." The adverb *slowly* can either be placed in its most natural position between the subject and the verb, or it can be taken to the beginning or to the end of the sentence. In some sentences there are even other possible positions for adverbs.

Earlier it was mentioned that one of the theories of case grammar was that in a particular sentence there is a preposition associated with each noun, although this preposition becomes deleted if the noun becomes a subject, a direct object, an indirect object, or an objective complement, as in the following sentences:

John repaired the motorcycle.
John loaded *hay* onto the truck.
John gave *Mary* the key.
He appointed John *treasurer.*

Corresponding to these sentences in which the prepositions are deleted are equivalent sentences with the preposition intact as follows:

The motorcycle was repaired *by John.*
John loaded the truck *with hay.*
John gave the key *to Mary.*
He appointed John *as treasurer.*

Nouns thus marked by prepositions are slightly more amenable to movement transformations than are those not marked by prepositions. Thus, *"With hay* John loaded the truck," while it is not elegant, is at least better than **"Hay* John loaded the truck." And *"To Mary* John gave the key," again though not elegant is better than **"Mary* John gave the key." Adverbial prepositional phrases have even fewer restrictions on their movement in sentences. "He fought Joe Louis *in Chicago"* can be changed to *"In Chicago* he fought Joe Louis." "He arrived *at ten o'clock"* can be changed to *"At ten o'clock* he arrived." "He opened the can *with care,"* can be changed to, *"With care* he opened the can." And finally, "He went to the hospital *because of a sore ankle"* can be changed to, *"Because of a sore ankle,* he went to the hospital." These sentence pairs illustrate that adverbial prepositional phrases have a freedom of movement whether they represent the semantic concepts of place, time, manner, or reason.   ·

In addition to adverbs and nouns (or prepositional phrases containing these nouns), adjectives can be moved about in a sentence. For example the sentence, "We visited the front of the lake," can be changed to "We visited the lake front," but there are more severe restrictions on the order of attributive adjectives than on some other structures. The following sentences illustrate what happens when adjectives are moved around:

I saw the man (who was) decrepit.
I saw the toy (which was) broken.
I saw the horse (which was) galloping.

If we delete the relative pronoun (*who* or *which*) and the essive verb (*was*), then a movement transformation is obligatory. We can say, "I saw the decrepit man," but not, "I saw the man decrepit." And "I saw the broken chair" and "I saw the galloping horse," express the meaning of the original sentences better than do, "I saw the chair broken," and "I saw the horse galloping." When one-word modifiers are expanded, then the movement transformation is not appropriate. That is, "I saw the man decrepit with age," "I saw the toy broken by the child," and "I saw the horse galloping through the meadow" are normal sentences while "I saw the decrepit-with-age man," "I saw the broken-by-the-child toy," and "I saw the galloping-through-the-meadow horse," are either awkward or unacceptable. Modification which comes before the head noun as in these last sentences (mostly individual words) is called left branching. Modification coming afterwards (mostly phrases and clauses) is called right branching.

Another type of movement transformation is called extraposition. It is through this transformation that such a sentence as "That he come is imperative" is related to "It is imperative that he come." This extraposition transformation has the effect of moving a *that* clause out of its normal subject position to the end of the sentence and putting in the word *it* to fill the space originally occupied by the *that* clause. A similar type of transformation is called *it* replacement. Through *it* replacement a sentence like "John appears to be shooting Bill" is changed to "It appears that John is shooting Bill." In this transformation, the infinitive *to be shooting Bill* is transformed into *that John is shooting Bill*. The subject of this structure (*John*) is lowered from the main (matrix) sentence, which leaves the main sentence without a subject for the verb *appears*. Since a subjectless verb is usually not tolerated in English, the expletive *it* comes to the rescue. There is a third type of transformation which is similar to both extraposition and *it* replacement. This is called subject raising. It is through subject raising that the following three sentences are related:

> It is easy to get this baby into these overalls.
> This baby is easy to get into these overalls.
> These overalls are easy to get this baby into.

It is through subject raising that a direct object (*this baby*) or the object of a preposition (*these overalls*) can become the subject of the sentence. If a different example is used, there are even more possibilities of subject raising:

> (For the mailman) to deliver the mail was difficult.
> To deliver the mail was difficult (for the mailman).
> The mail was difficult (for the mailman) to deliver.
> It was difficult (for the mailman) to deliver the mail.

Notice that when neither the direct object nor the object of the preposition is raised to subject position, there is no noun to fill this position, and this vacancy must therefore be filled by the expletive *it*. Another word which functions as an expletive in English and can therefore fill in vacancies in the subject slot left by movement transformations is the word *there*. In relating the sentence, "Five students were involved in the robbery" with "There were five students involved in the robbery," we must realize that the subject noun phrase *five students* is moved out of its normal subject position and that the expletive *there* is taking the grammatical place of the subject.

Another type of movement transformation is negative raising. In explaining this, we will first consider a verb which does *not* allow negative raising. The sentence, "I didn't require him to come" is very different in meaning from the sentence "I required him not to come." Therefore a linguist would not want to say that these two sentences are related to each other through any transformation. But now consider two superficially similar sentences. Compare "I didn't want him to come," with "I wanted him not to come." These two sentences *are* paraphrases of each other, and for these two sentences, therefore, we would want to say that they are transformationally related. Notice that in the sentence, "I didn't want him to come," it is the *coming* not the *wanting* that is semantically negated. The sentence, "I didn't want him to come," does not mean that "I didn't want something." In fact, it means the opposite. The speaker wanted something. What the speaker wanted was "for him *not* to come." But contrast, "I didn't want him to come," with "I didn't require him to come." Whereas in the first sentence the domain of *not* is the subordinate verb rather than the main verb, in the second sentence the domain of *not* is the main rather than the subordinate verb. This fact can be best accounted for by assuming that the sentence, "I didn't want him to come" is derived from the sentence, "I wanted him not to come" by the meaning-preserving negative raising transformation. On the other hand, "I didn't require him to come," is not derived from "I required him not to come" by any transformation, since these two sentences do not have the same meaning. In English, the verbs *believe, would like,* and *think* are like *want* in that they are verbs which allow negative raising. *Happy, hope,* and *try* are like *require* in that they do not allow negative raising. The term "negative raising" is a general term which can be used to describe this phenomenon in a variety of languages. A term sometimes used specifically for English is "not transportation" or "not hopping," which simply refers to the fact that the *not* is moved around in the sentence.

Another movement transformation in English is passivization. It is this transformation which relates, "A car hit John" with "John was hit by a car." The effect of the passive transformation is to change or demote the subject of a sentence into the object of a preposition, and to promote the direct object of a sentence to subject position. Now consider a sequence like "Mary gave John the money" and its passive counterpart, "John was given the money by Mary." And compare this passive sentence with "John received the money from Mary." Is it not true that *was given by* is in some sense equivalent to *received from*? For the moment, let us consider *receive* to be the unmarked or lexical passive of *give*. Words like this, which are a special type of converse, reverse the subject-object roles of two noun phrases. The *give-receive* pair are not alone in this respect as can be seen by the following examples:

VERB:	SYNTACTIC PASSIVE:	LEXICAL PASSIVE:
think	be thought	seem
sell	be sold	buy
give	be given	receive/take
precede	be preceded	follow
own/possess	be owned	belong
regard	be regarded	strike
frighten	be frightened	fear
enjoy	be enjoyed	amuse
like	be liked	please
dislike	be disliked	annoy

In these examples the syntactic passive has the same meaning as the lexical passive. For example:

I regard her as being less than bright.
She is regarded as being less than bright (by me).
She strikes me as being less than bright.

all communicate basically the same thing. And if "I precede John," then "John is preceded by me," and this is the same as "John follows me." Or if "I own a house," then it is also true that "A house is owned by me" and "A house belongs to me." Each of the verbs in the left column above has the same meaning as its lexical passive in the right column, the only difference being that the subject and object roles are reversed, just as they would be if the passive were formed syntactically. The last four sets: *frighten-fear, enjoy-amuse, like-please,* and *dislike-annoy* are said to be related to each other through the psych-movement transformation. This works with psychological verbs and verbs of perception which have two forms. One of them takes the Experiencer first and the Object second, as in "I enjoyed the play." The other form takes the Object first and the Experiencer second, as in "The play amused me."

There are other sets of words which are neither antonyms nor lexical passives. These include such words as *talk-say-speak-tell, rob-steal,* and *blame on-blame for.* These are not lexical passives because the subject and object roles are not reversed. They occur with different types of complements, but all of them nevertheless have the same subject, as can be seen in the following examples:

I talked (all day).
I said, "He is an idiot."
I spoke to John. I spoke French (to John). I spoke.
I told John (that we might not come).

These sentences illustrate that the verb *talk* is intransitive, *say* is transitive requiring a direct object, *speak* is either intransitive or transitive with a language as the direct object and with an optional preposition marked indirect object, and *tell* is a slightly different type of transitive. But because the subject is always the same for these particular words, they are neither antonyms nor lexical passives of each other. The same is true for *rob* versus *steal*. Notice that both "I robbed the First National Bank of $500" and "I stole $500 from the First National Bank" have the same subject, although they have different types of complements. Consider also, "I blamed Mary for the accident" versus "I blamed the accident on Mary."

All of these words whether they are antonyms, lexical passives, or merely words requiring different complements may be thought of as paraphrases of each other because they refer to the same real-world state, event, or activity.

There are a number of other sentences which are said to be related to each other through various transformations. For example, the declarative sentence, "You will shut the door" is said to be related to its negative counterpart, "You won't shut the door," by the negative transformation. This same sentence is said to be related to its interrogative counterpart, "Will you shut the door?", by the question transformation and to its imperative counterpart, "Shut the door!", by the imperative transformation. And sentences like "Don't shut the door" and "Won't you shut the door" are said to be derived from this same sentence by the application of both the negative and the imperative transformations for the first example, and the negative and question transformations for the second. It can hardly be denied that an affirmative sentence like "You will shut the door" has a striking superficial resemblance to its negative counterpart. Probably the best way to talk about these sentences is to say that a negative sentence is transformationally related to its affirmative counterpart. But we must also realize that an affirmative sentence does not relate to the real world in the same way that its negative counterpart does. An affirmative sentence is true if and only if its negative counterpart is *false*. Question and imperative sentences are also different from their declarative counterparts in their truth values. A declarative sentence is a statement of fact, while an imperative is a request for a certain kind of action, and a question is a request for a verbal action or response. If someone says, "You will shut the door," they are indicating something which *will* happen in the future, but if it is stated as a question the resultant response might be either affirmative or negative, and if stated as a command the resultant action may or may not take place. Therefore, it must be realized that the negative, question, and imperative transformations are different from the other transformations discussed in this chapter because they are not paraphrase transformations. The resulting sentences are structurally related to each other, but semantically they are quite different.

Let us now go from movement transformations to reduction and deletion transformations. We've already mentioned that such transformations are meaning-preserving because they relate to the real world in exactly the same way, except that there is a tendency for expressions that have been reduced to be vaguer than sentences which have not been reduced. First let us consider a series of transformations that have the effect of reducing sentences to the level of dependent clauses or phrases. There are five such transformations in English. The transformation which changes the sentence "We own a house on 16th Street" to ". . . that we own a house on 16th Street" is called the that-clause transformation. This transformation merely places the word *that* in front of a sentence to make it a dependent clause so that it can function as a substantive, i.e., a noun replacement. This in itself does not show any reduction, but what happens with this kind of clause is that it is usually combined with another sentence and in this way saves repetition of the subject.

Another transformation that changes a sentence into a dependent clause is the relative transformation, the application of which will change a sentence like "We own a house on 16th Street" to ". . . where we own a house" or ". . . what we own on 16th Street." This transformation does two things. It changes some constituent, a noun, adverb, determiner, etc., into a relative pronoun, and it takes this relative pronoun to the beginning of the clause.

The difference between a relative clause such as ". . . whose horse he saw" and the question "Whose horse did he see?" is that the first structure has only had the relative clause transformation applied to it, while the second has undergone both the relative clause transformation and the question transformation. Since the question transformation carries with it the meaning of "requesting a verbal response," there is a difference in the meaning of these two structures. Also the relative clause has an antecedent, even if it's only in the mind of the speaker, while the relative question does not. This is semantically predictable: the question relative pronoun could not have an antecedent because this is what the listener is expected to provide in his response.

Then there are the gerundive, action, and infinitival transformations. The sentence "John bought a new home" can be changed by the action transformation into ". . . the buying of a new home." The gerundive transformation changes it into ". . . John's buying (of) a new home," and the infinitive transformation changes it into, ". . . (for John) to buy a new home." As the name implies, the action transformation is a possible transformation only for sentences which indicate an action. The gerundive and infinitival transformations, however, are appropriate for any sentences.

In conclusion, the that-clause, relative, gerundive, action, and infinitival transformations have the effect of demoting a sentence to the rank of dependent clause or phrase. The resultant action phrases or *that* clauses are then in an appropriate form to be used as noun substitutes. The resultant relative clauses, gerundive phrases, or infinitival phrases can be used either as noun substitutes or as noun modifiers.

Reduction and deletion are actually two parts of the same process: a section of a sentence is deleted, and the full sentence is reduced. In a way, deletion can also be thought of as reduction to the point of zero. Since reduction and deletion are actually two aspects of the same thing, it is logical that the same semantic constraint would apply to both. This constraint is that there must be an antecedent in order for reduction or deletion to occur. The term which is most often used by grammarians to describe reduction is *pronominalization*. This is misleading because it isn't just nouns (i.e., nominalizations) that can be reduced. A better term would be *pro-forms* because this would indicate the variety; for example adverbs are reduced to *when*, determiners to *which*, possessive nouns and adjectives to *whose*, verb phrases to *do so*, and sentences to *this fact*, etc. In English there are a number of different types of pronouns, including personal pronouns, *(he, him, I, me, we, us, you, they, them, she*, and *her)*, the relative pronouns *(who, which, that, when, where, why, how)*, the reflexive pronouns *(himself, myself, ourselves, yourselves, themselves*, and *herself)* and intensive pronouns, which have the same form as the reflexive pronouns. The word *himself* is a reflexive pronoun in the sentence "He cut himself," but an intensive pronoun in the sentence "He built the house himself." There are also cooperative pronouns like *together* and reciprocal pronouns like *each other*. All these pro-forms enable speakers and writers to make use of the principles of reduction.

Let us now look at what happens if the reduction goes all the way resulting in a deletion. One of the most common types of deletion is known as equi-NP deletion which simply means that an equivalent noun phrase is deleted. In this process two juxtaposed sentences like "This is the boy" and "John embarrassed the boy" will be combined. The second sentence will be converted into a relative clause and inserted as a modifier of the first sentence with the result being "This is the boy who(m) John embarrassed." The second occurrence of *the boy* is reduced to its pronominal form *who(m)*. If we go one step further this pronoun is lost altogether so that the resultant sentence is, "This is the boy John embarrassed." This sentence actually went through two steps. First was equi-NP reduction, and then was equi–NP deletion. Notice that in neither the sentence containing reduction nor in the sentence containing deletion was any information lost since it was all recoverable from the antecedent. In the example we have been considering, it is possible either to reduce to a pronoun or to reduce to nothing. But the sentence "The boy *who* arrived yesterday is my friend," which is a combined form of "The boy is my friend" and "The boy arrived yesterday," allows reduction but not deletion. The pronoun *who* must be left in the sentence. In another example the deletion of the second NP is obligatory. When the sentences, "John expected something" and "John will go to school" are combined into, "John expected (John or himself) to go to school," the normal resultant sentence is "John expected to go to school." The degree of deletion allowed or demanded is mainly determined by the choice of verb.

We've already shown how prepositional phrases and adverbs can optionally be deleted from English sentences. We will now look at the effect of equi-constituent deletion on conjunction. Consider the following pairs of sentences and their conjoined forms. The redundant information is italicized.

John *saw the accident.*
Mary *saw the accident.*   John and Mary *saw the accident.*

John ate an apple.
John ate a pear.   *John ate* an apple and a pear.

John ate an apple.
John smashed a pear.   *John* ate an apple and smashed a pear.

John has lived in Chicago.
John has lived in New York.   *John has lived in* Chicago and New York.

They elected John secretary.
They elected John treasurer.   *They elected John* secretary and
          treasurer.

I gave Mary *a dollar.*
I gave Bill *a dollar.*   *I gave* Mary and Bill *a dollar.*

I read a book.
John studied.   I read a book and John studied.

The process shown here should be obvious. There is no reason to say exactly the same thing twice; therefore in the sentence on the right the redundant material is deleted, and whatever is left, i.e., the nonredundant material, is conjoined. The examples above show the conjunction of subjects, direct objects, verb phrases, objects of prepositions, objective complements, indirect objects, and complete sentences. Complete sentence conjunction is the result when there is no redundancy at all as in the last example. We should mention that for some of the sentences on the right there are two readings. For example, "I gave Mary and Bill a dollar," could mean either that "I gave Mary a dollar" and "I gave Bill a dollar," which would represent two actions and would mean that two dollars were given, or "I gave Mary and Bill a dollar" might represent only one action in which one dollar was given for them to share. Only the first of these possibilities is derived by a conjunction of two sentences. In the other case when there is only one action the sentence is basic and is not derived from anything. The sentence, "They elected John secretary and treasurer," illustrates this point further. If secretary and treasurer is one office, rather than two, the sentence is not the result of the conjunction of two more-basic sentences. Or consider the sentence, "John and Mary saw the accident." In one reading, the word *together* can be placed on the end resulting in the sentence, "John and Mary saw the accident together." In this reading a single action took place, and the sentence is basic as it stands and is therefore not derived by the conjunction of two more basic sentences.

Gapping is the name given to another kind of deletion transformation where redundant information is left out and the resulting sentence parts are brought together to close the gap. In the sentence, "I ordered pumpkin pie, and Tom apple pie," the last part of the sentence does not contain a verb. Yet any native speaker would know that "Tom apple pie" in this particular context means "Tom ordered apple pie." The verb is recoverable because of the general principle that only recoverable information is deleted. Therefore the listener assumes that this verb must be the same as the one immediately preceding.

Sluicing is another deletion transformation. It is through the sluicing transformation that the verb phrase of a sentence can be gradually shortened as follows:

> John should not have been working the midnight shift, but Jack should have been working the midnight shift.

> John should not have been working the midnight shift, but Jack should have been working.

> John should not have been working the midnight shift, but Jack should have been.

> John should not have been working the midnight shift, but Jack should have.

> John should not have been working the midnight shift, but Jack should.

All of the sentences in this set are grammatical; however, the first two seem to us to be less stylistically acceptable than the others, probably because too much redundant material is retained.

LEXICAL PARAPHRASE:

In discussing antonymy we developed the idea of semantic continuums in relation to the specific features of words. Antonyms were at opposite ends of these continuums. Synonyms appear on the same continuums, but rather than being at opposite ends they are as close as possible to each other. For example, *usually, often, frequently,* and *generally* are all synonyms of each other, as are such words as *turnpike, freeway, thruway,* and *highway.* However, no two synonyms have exactly the same meaning. They may differ from each other in style, e.g., *castle-palace;* in geographical dialect, e.g., *subway-metro-tube-underground;* in formality, e.g., *fatigued-exhausted-tired out-worn out-beat-tuckered out-pooped;* in vulgarity, e.g., *breast-tits;* in attitude of the speaker, e.g., *policeman-fuzz;* and in many other ways.

The vast majority of words have enough distinguishing features that they are not really synonyms, even though they have exactly the same case frame and therefore belong to the same lexical category. We will look at words of motion, for example, and try to determine how many synonyms there are among words which indicate the movement of a person or animal from one place to another via a certain route in which the legs are the means of locomotion. Words of this type can be grouped into sets that have certain similarities and are therefore somewhat synonymous. Such words as *clomp, tramp, plod,* and *stomp* indicate a slow, deliberate, burdened type of locomotion. *Ramble, romp,* and *gambol* represent a spirited vigorous fast movement. A slow, purposeless and casual kind of locomotion is represented by such words as *stroll, rove, amble, meander, wander,* and *saunter. Stagger, stumble,* and *limp* have an additional feature of abnormal uncontrolled walking. If the walking is unusually sharp, crisp, and vigorous the words *prance, promenade, stride,* and *strut* might apply. Walking in a group with everyone doing the same thing at the same time could be classified as either *march, dance, promenade,* or *goosestep,* although these words have additional specific features so that they are not synonymous in all ways. Also troops can *jog* and *double-time* together. Other words indicating a fast kind of movement include *run, canter, trot, gallop,* and *lope.* The expressions *dash* and *sprint* usually refer to a competitive kind of short race with a definite goal in mind, while *scamper* is not goal oriented. *Leap, jump, hop,* and *skip* are sometimes considered synonyms. Of these the first two are more nearly synonymous because they represent a single movement in which height or distance is the intended result. *Hopping* and *skipping* on the other hand can be done for a longer distance by repeating the action over and over. Some speakers feel that there is a horizontal-vertical distinction between *leap* and *jump*, but other speakers feel that the difference is one of formality with *leap* being more formal than *jump*. We might ask if the plain ordinary word *walk* is a synonym of all these words. Rather than being a synonym, it is a cover term because it is too vague; it does not have specific features which can be compared with the specific features of these other words. This is just one indication that synonymy is not an easy thing to deal with.

Before leaving synonymy, let us consider some examples of words which have different meanings, for example *hard, thin, light* and *high*. Because of their different meanings, these four words have different sets of synonyms. And as might be expected they have different sets of antonyms based on the same distinguishing features as represented below:

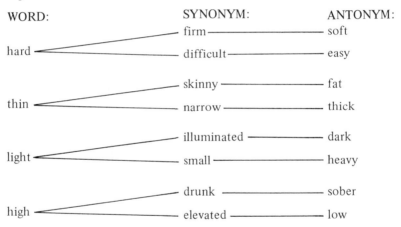

WORD:	SYNONYM:	ANTONYM:
hard	firm	soft
	difficult	easy
thin	skinny	fat
	narrow	thick
light	illuminated	dark
	small	heavy
high	drunk	sober
	elevated	low

Still another problem is that certain words may have different strict subcategorization or selection restrictions even though they are otherwise synonymous. For example, a person is six feet *tall* but a mound of dirt is six feet *high*. A horse *gallops* but a deer or an elephant moving at the same speed *runs* not *gallops*. A person is *young* while a car is *new*, but after a few years they are both *old*. You might buy a *second-hand* lawnmower and a *used* car, but a house is just a house. And while your car might need *tuning up*, your house will need *fixing up*.

Turning to a different kind of synonymy, some linguists have suggested that such syntactically different expressions as *use* and *with* or *have, of,* and *is* are synonyms of each other. For example the communication is the same in "I *used* cement to make it" and "I made it *with* cement." The communication is also the same in "John *has* the book," "The book *of* John's ...," and "The book *is* John's."

Now let us turn to the most important and widespread type of paraphrase which is that of lexical incorporation. It is also the least understood aspect of paraphrase. The verb *cemented* in the sentence, "John *cemented* his driveway," is quite clearly a word which contains lexical incorporation. This sentence can be paraphrased by the sentence, "John covered his driveway with *cement.*" *Cemented* in the first sentence is equivalent to *covered with cement* in the second. Through the process of incorporation, the three words *covered with cement* become amalgamated into the single word *cemented.* The verb *cemented* is an example of transparent incorporation, so called because we can still see the word that has been incorporated. The verb *slap* is an example of opaque incorporation. This verb is related to the expression, "hit with the flat of the hand," but there is nothing visible in the word *slap* to indicate that the hitting is done with the flat of the hand. It is because the incorporated concept or word is hidden that this kind of incorporation is called opaque.

There are many different types of expressions that can be incorporated into the verb as seen in the following chart:

CATEGORY OF ITEM INCORPORATED	NON-INCORPORATED EXPRESSION:	INCORPORATED EXPRESSION:
Instrument	to hit with a hammer	to hammer
Material	to cover with gravel	to gravel
Object	to drive a nail	to nail
Location	to put in a box	to box
Time	to keep track of the time	to time
Body part	to touch with the lips	to kiss
Manner	to walk in an abnormal manner	to stagger
Speed	to move rapidly	to zip (along)
Power	to hit hard repeatedly	to pound

It is not hard to see how this list could be greatly extended.

The elements inchoative and cause are also often lexically incorporated into the verb. The expression *learn* can be broken down into *become knowledgeable*, and *teach* can be broken down into *cause to become knowledgeable* or *cause to learn*. There are many such examples. Or consider the verb *resemble* in "Harry resembles an ape." The fact that this sentence has a paraphrase, "I perceive Harry as being similar to an ape," indicates that *resemble* is actually a shorthand form of *perceive . . . similar*. This process can be described as either lexical incorporation or lexical decomposition, depending on whether the process is viewed synthetically or analytically. In order to see the process more clearly, we will look at an entire semantic set of words and analyze how words which are semantically very similar can be distinguished from each other. For this exercise, we will consider verbs of judging which include *accuse, admit, apologize, blame, castigate, chastise, chide, commend, concede, condemn, confess, credit, criticize, deny, excuse, forgive, guilty, judge, justify, praise, rationalize, regret, responsible, scold,* etc. Any native speaker who has not formally studied the semantic composition of such expressions will probably be able to indicate that for all of them there is an act committed and of course a person who has committed the act. When sentences are spoken using these words there is a speaker and a listener and usually a third person who is the accused. The first person speaker is usually the one who either evaluates the act or asserts who is responsible for the act. With these words having all of these things in common even a well-educated and sophisticated native speaker would be hard pressed to explain the differences among them. However he would probably be perfectly able to use them. Since the duty of a linguist is to state explicitly what native speakers know implicitly about their language, we will attempt to reconsider these verbs of judging, this time concentrating on their differences rather than their similarities.

The first thing to notice about such verbs is the number of arguments that are in their case frames and the linear position of the arguments in the sentence as first, second, or third position. We will begin with those verbs of judging in which the judge comes first, the defendant comes second, and the action comes last, as follows:

JUDGE:	PREDICATE:	DEFENDANT ACTOR:	ACTION:
1. John	credited	Mary	with studying hard.
2. John	commended	Mary	for studying hard.
3. John	praised	Mary	for studying hard.
4. John	excused	Mary	for studying hard.
5. John	forgave	Mary	for studying hard.
6. John	condemned	Mary	for studying hard.
7. John	criticized	Mary	for studying hard.
8. John	blamed	Mary	for studying hard.
9. John	accused	Mary	of studying hard.
10. John	castigated	Mary	for studying hard.
11. John	chastised	Mary	for studying hard.
12. John	reprimanded	Mary	for studying hard.
13. John	scolded	Mary	for studying hard.
14. John	chided	Mary	for studying hard.

These sentences, in addition to all having the same arguments, and having them in the same order, are organized in such a way that the words most like each other are placed together. In the first three sentences (credit, commend, praise), John judges Mary's action to be good. In the second two sentences (excuse, forgive), he has judged her action to be acceptable, although it was first considered bad. In the rest of the sentences (condemned, criticized, blamed, accused, castigated, chastised, reprimanded, scolded, chided), he has judged her action to be bad. If we look even more closely, we can make further distinctions to show that none of these words are absolute synonyms. In sentence (1), for example (credit), John presupposes that the action is good and states or asserts that Mary was responsible for the action. In sentences (2) and (3), John presupposes that Mary was responsible for the action. What he states or asserts is that the action is good. Commend and praise are probably as close as we will get to true synonyms, although some people feel that commend is stronger. Forgive and excuse are similarly synonymous with the difference being again a matter of strength. If John forgives Mary for something, this implies that what she did was very bad, whereas if he excuses her, this implies that she committed a minor offense. These two words are similar to justify, rationalize, and apologize in that with all five of these words a bad action becomes an acceptable action. However they differ in that with *excuse* and *forgive* it is the judge (John) who reevaluates the action, while for *justify, rationalize,* and *apologize* it is the defendant (Mary). This is reflected in the surface ordering of the arguments where John appears as the surface structure subject when he is doing the reevaluating.

In sentences (6), (7), and (8), John judges Mary's action to be bad, and this remains his opinion throughout the sentences as shown by *condemn, criticize,* and *blame. Blame* is different from *criticize* and *condemn* in that *blame* can be simply a mental attitude while *criticize* and *condemn* are speech or writing acts with *condemn* being the stronger term.

Now let us consider sentences (9) through (14). Sentence (9) *(accuse)* differs from the others *(castigate, chastise, reprimand, scold,* and *chide)* in that in the sentence with *accuse* John asserts that Mary is responsible for the action. In the other sentences, this information is merely presupposed. These five words are very similar in meaning. For all of them, John presupposes that Mary is responsible for the action and that the action is bad. All of them indicate that John was performing a special kind of speech act in which he tells Mary that her action was bad. *Castigate* is the strongest word, *chastise* comes next, followed by *reprimand,* then *scold,* and then the relatively weak *chide.*

Now let's return to the verbs where the defendant *(Mary)* comes before the verb and the judge *(John)* comes after the verb as in the following sentences:

DEFENDANT: JUDGE: ACTOR:	PREDICATE:	LISTENER:	ACTION:
15. Mary	apologized	to John	for studying hard.
16. Mary	rationalized	to John	for studying hard.
17. Mary	confessed	to John	that she studied hard.
18. Mary	admitted	to John	that she studied hard.
19. Mary	conceded	to John	that she studied hard.

The verbs *apologize* and *rationalize* from sentences (15) and (16) are very similar. In both of these sentences Mary presupposes that she was responsible for the action and that the action was bad; and in both of these sentences she somehow makes up for the badness of the action with some sort of oral response. The difference between the two verbs is that *apologize* is a speech act directed to John, admitting guilt, while *rationalize* is a speech and mental act directed to both John and Mary and not admitting guilt.

Confess, admit, and *concede* from sentences (17), (18), and (19) are more similar to each other than are *apologize* and *rationalize*. For these three verbs, Mary presupposes that she is responsible for the action and she asserts that the action was bad. These words all indicate speech acts, and they differ from each other only in strength, with *confess* being the strongest, *admit* being the next strongest, and *concede* being the weakest of the three.

There are two other verbs of judging with three-place predicates in which the defendant *(Mary)* comes before the judge *(John)*. These differ from the above sentences in that the action as well as the defendant comes before the judge. In other words, for this class of verbs, the judge *(John)* comes last.

DEFENDANT: JUDGE: ACTOR:	PREDICATE:	ACTION:	LISTENER:
20. Mary	justified	her studying hard	to John.
21. Mary	denied	studying hard	to Johnn.

For both sentence (20) and sentence (21), John presupposed that Mary was responsible for the action and that the action was bad. In sentence (20) *(justify)*, Mary asserts that the action was acceptable; whereas in sentence (21) *(deny)*, Mary as well as John presuppose that the action was bad, and her assertion is that she did not do it. Another difference between these two words is that *justify* represents a mental, and perhaps a speech act, while *deny* represents a speech act.

Finally let us consider some verbs of judging with two-place predicates such as the following:

DEFENDANT: ACTOR:	PREDICATE:	ACTION:
22. Mary	judged	that she studied hard.
23. Mary	regretted	studying hard.
24. Mary	was guilty	of studying hard.
25. Mary	was responsible	for studying hard.

All four of these verbs represent mental acts on Mary's part. In sentence (22), the verb *judge* asserts merely that Mary was responsible for the action. There are no presuppositions on anyone's part that the action is either good or bad. This verb is very similar to such verbs as *assume, feel, believe, realize,* and many others which are not considered in this discussion. In sentence (23) *(regret),* Mary presupposes that she was responsible for the action and asserts that she is sorry, which means, of course, that the action must have been bad. In sentence (24) *(guilty)* and sentence (25) *(responsible),* it is not Mary but rather the speaker of the sentence who is asserting that Mary is responsible. In sentence (24) *(guilty),* but not sentence (25) *(responsible),* the speaker makes the further assertion that Mary's action was bad.

What we have been attempting to do is to suggest a method of contrastive lexical decomposition. It would be foolish, of course, to take a lexical item and to break it down into all its components since this is a futile task. Lexical items have so many components that such an exercise would result in total frustration and probably wouldn't produce a great many valuable insights into the nature of the lexicon. If, on the other hand, we consider only those components of a particular lexical item which are relevant in contrasting it with another lexical item, we have a principled way of restricting focus to those features relevant to a particular purpose.

X. Universals

The kind of semantic theory treated in this book has contributed to a renewed interest in linguistic universals. When grammarians and linguists were concerned basically with surface structures, it appeared that languages, even those closely related. were very different from each other. But as linguists became more interested in semantics, they discovered that languages are actually very much alike, and they began to concentrate on the similarities rather than the differences. In other words, they became interested in language universals, of which there are many. And in addition to discovering these universals, they began trying to figure out the reasons behind these similarities in languages.

Four basic explanations for linguistic universals have been proposed: (1) that they happened accidentally and independently; (2) that these features were aspects of a single language from which all world languages derived; (3) that there is a great deal of linguistic pre-programming in the human brain that makes these universals innate; and/or (4) that there are real-world constraints on the nature of human languages.

It is likely that there are at least some linguistic universals which fall partially into each of these categories. In this chapter we won't discuss such things as language acquisition and the fact that, if there is a triggering stimulus of language, all children seem to learn to speak at basically the same rate regardless of IQ, motivation, training, quality of language heard, etc. We're also disregarding human preference for certain types of transformations, e.g., left or right adjoining over other types of transformation, e.g., self-embedding, because these phenomena must be studied with the help of the psychologist, the neurophysicist, and possibly the mathematician, and this kind of in-depth study is beyond the scope of the present book.

It is in vogue for linguists to agree with Chomsky that there is a great deal of pre-programming in the brain, and undoubtedly this accounts for much of what is universal across languages. However there is also something to be said for the constraints which are present as a result of real-world conditions outside of the brain and the principle of efficiency in communication. At any rate, it is clear that the majority of non-accidental universals are those which are semantically based, whether they are innate or real-world controlled. This means that we would not expect to find linguistic universals in the areas of phonology, morphology, syntax, or writing since these are all surface structure, language-dependent levels. It is because of this and also because of the numerous counterexamples that we would reject the claim of some linguists about the universality of what is called the A over A principle. This principle states that if you have a certain type of constituent appearing in a sentence under the same type of constituent it cannot be moved out from under that constituent. For example the English sentence, "You would approve of John's excessive drinking of beer," is acceptable, as is, "What would you approve of?" With this latter question the noun phrase has been taken out of the prepositional phrase, and this is acceptable. But when the noun phrase is taken out of the noun phrase, an unacceptable sentence results, *"What would you approve of John's excessive drinking of?" This is Chomsky's example, and it illustrates a principle which holds true in English and in many other languages. But it is our opinion that it is too language specific to be considered a universal. The same holds true for the "Cross Over" principle which is also claimed to be a universal. This principle states that a constituent in a sentence may not be moved past another constituent having the same referent. For example, in English "John shaved himself," is acceptable, while *"Himself was shaved by John," is unacceptable, but the Hiligaynon language uses an anaphoric form before the referrant.

But now let us turn to the kinds of things which appear to us to be universals. First, all languages have phonetic assimilation and phonetic dissimilation. These are unusual examples of universals in two respects; first they appear to be surface structure universals in the area of phonetics, and second, since they are opposite processes it would appear that whatever justifies one would invalidate the other. However, let's look at assimilation and dissimilation as semantic processes rather than as phonological processes. If a person ennunciates perfectly, pronouncing every syllable distinctly, articulating every sound, and not merging any sounds into any other sounds, he will be forced to take a great deal of extra time to do this. His communication is therefore impeded by the fact that he can't talk rapidly. He is therefore able to utter only half or a third as many sentences as he would be able to utter with approximate, rather than precise, articulation. The function of assimilation is really to get as much speech into a given amount of time as possible.

Now let us look at the opposite process of dissimilation from a semantic point of view. If sounds are so similar that they cannot be distinguished, and if this results in a problem of understanding, dissimilation often takes place. Therefore, while assimilation is for speed and efficiency, dissimilation is for clarity, and these two processes work against each other in all languages—but always toward the same goal—maximum communication. Consider two examples from English. The -s suffix, whether it signals plural, possessive, or third person singular present indicative, and the -d suffix, whether it signals past tense or past participle, are voiced or voiceless according to the preceding sound as in boys contrasted with hats and sewed contrasted with jumped. But where the assimilation would be too close, as in bus-s, or trott-t, a vowel has to be inserted for clarity, yielding buses and trotted.

The ways in which assimilation and dissimilation can be accomplished are universal in character and extremely finite in number. In this case, the universals are the result of an extremely limited number of articulators that can be moved closer together or farther apart. We can move our tongues, lips, vocal chords, and velics. As far as the tongue is concerned, assimilation and dissimilation can be described in terms of raising, lowering, backing, and fronting; as to the lips they can be rounded or unrounded; the vocal chords can be voiced or unvoiced; and the velic can be open, producing nasalization, or closed.

All languages have deletion and reduction transformations as described for English in Chapter IX. It is universal that when forms are reduced or pronominalized there is a reduction in specificity in that the pronoun always contains fewer semantic features than does the noun it replaces. The pronouns *which* or *that,* for example, do not contain as many semantic features as the words they replace, e.g., *horse,* or *cow,* or *tree.*

In all languages pronominalization is a reduction in the number of semantic features, and deletion is merely a further reduction to the point that nothing is left. Both reduction transformations and deletion transformations normally have the same condition, i.e., there is an antecedent from which the deleted semantic features can be recovered. This "antecedent" need not be in the linguistic context. The pronouns *I* and *you* do not need formal antecedents because they are already explicit in meaning the speaker and listener respectively. Only third person pronouns, in addition to nouns which are automatically third person in normal usage, need antecedents. Even third person pronouns can get along without formal antecedents if the referent is in the immediate social context.

But as a matter of fact, there are actually three conditions of deletion or reduction rather than just one. Material is deleted or reduced if it is recoverable, if it is irrelevant, or if it is unknown. These are all perfectly logical conditions, and all serve to make communication more efficient. If material is redundant, then nothing is lost by deletion, and succinctness is gained. If something is irrelevant, then if not deleted it would impede communication by taking up some time and by confusing the issue. And finally, if material is unknown, then the speaker has no choice but to delete it or refer to it with a vague word containing very few specific semantic features. So the effect of deletion is similar to the effect of assimilation. By getting rid of redundant or irrelevant material we are able to put more communication into a given amount of time.

We agree with Chomsky that although particular transformations are language specific and are therefore not linguistic universals, there are certain transformational operations, such as inversion, deletion, addition, substitution, etc. which are indeed universal. These transformations are structure dependent, that is, they operate only on constituents such as parts of speech, phrases, and clauses. But this fact does not tell us whether or not these things are innate. Nor do we have evidence to show that transformations must be ordered, and that recursiveness should be stated in terms of transformations cycling back upon themselves. It may be that transformations do not have a psychological reality, whereby, for example, the underlying representation of a passive sentence is derived from the underlying representation of an active sentence by certain formal operations. There is no question that active sentences are related to passive sentences, and the grammatical transformation may be a convenient way to show this relationship, but this certainly does not mean that the transformation is innate or even that it is universal; it may merely be a convenient fiction like the phoneme which has been shown to be a very useful notational and pedagogical tool, even though speech sounds do not actually occur as individual phonemes.

Even if the grammatical transformation does exist in the human mind, this does not explain paraphrase relationships in the narrow sense. This is obviously true when such transformations as negative and question are considered, for it is clear that these types of transformations do not hold meaning constant. And even the so-called "paraphrase" transformations, while they do not change truth value, do indeed change focus, presuppositions, scope, pronominalization, and the distribution of old and new information.

Various kinds of locutionary acts are also universals. All languages, for example, have questions, i.e., requests for information; commands, i.e., requests for action; statements, i.e., giving of information, etc., although the surface signals may differ greatly from language to language. Questions may be indicated by word inversion, by inflection, by a particle, etc., and as in English there is not always a close match between form and meaning, so that a question form might be used to command or state while a statement form may be used to command or question, etc.

All languages also have ways of foregrounding or backgrounding information, though again different languages have very different ways of doing this. Although there is obviously conflicting evidence, we would like to suggest that the subject-predicate word order is a universal, or at least a universal tendency. The subject-predicate distinction, which is called various things by various people states the basic relationship between old and new information. It is the function of the subject to establish a field of discourse for the sentence, and it is the function of the predicate to say something about this field of discourse. It seems very logical, then, to suggest the subject-predicate order as a universal tendency, so that the sentence goes from the known (subject) to the unknown (predicate).

All human beings, no matter when or where they live in the world, are able to make basically the same kind of judgments about language. Any grammar which is designed to reflect linguistic competence must treat such matters, and since humans can make these types of judgments regardless of which language they speak, these judgments are language universals. For one example, all people are aware of certain logical relationships such as the part-whole relationship, and this has linguistic consequences. Notice that we can say, "I bought a new car, but the horn didn't work." Ordinarily it is not possible to use the definite article *the* unless we make the noun specific either immediately before, as in "I bought a new horn, but the damn thing won't blow," or immediately afterwards as in "The horn which I just bought doesn't work." But in the first sentence, "I bought a new car, but the horn didn't work," we don't have to say anything about the horn to qualify it for use with the definite article because we have mentioned *car,* and we know that ordinarily a horn is an integral part of a car.

All people, regardless of language, are also aware of the conditions outside of the linguistic context that affect the appropriateness of a sentence. In linguistic literature these requirements imposed by the real world on the language are termed *happiness conditions, felicity conditions,* or *extrinsic modifiers.* A sentence which fails to meet these external conditions is termed inappropriate or unhappy. For example, we cannot use the imperative sentence "Close the door!" unless there is a door and unless there would be no confusion as to what door is meant, and unless the door is open, and unless the listener is awake, and understands English, and would be inclined to do what the speaker told him to do. All these things are presuppositions of the imperative sentence "Close the door!" They are facts which the speaker must suppose before he is able to utter the command, "Close the door!" in good faith. Notice that the negative command, "Don't close the door!" has practically the same presuppositions (happiness conditions) as the affirmative command.

A related universal would be reference reality. Consider a sentence like, "The king of the United States is a bad fellow." This sentence is neither true nor false but rather *inappropriate,* since the presuppositions (that there is one and only one king of the United States) are incorrect, then the assertion (that he is a bad fellow) can not be judged. An assertion is therefore seen to be either true, false, or inappropriate. Another possibility exists, and this is that the "king of the United States," might be a referring expression based either on lack of knowledge about United States government on the part of the speaker or on a facetious type of reference which implies that although the United States doesn't have a king, we may have a person who acts like one. Because of the creative nature of the human mind, probably all languages have referring expressions for things that don't exist and never have, yet these referring expressions are often very precise and well specified. Educated speakers of English know what kinds of modification and predication are appropriate for such referents as *dragons, unicorns, Santa Claus,* the *Easter Bunny, elves, gremlins,* and the god *Neptune.* Probably all cultures and therefore all languages have some pretty standard agreement on the semantic features of some of their non-referring terms.

All languages contain implication, although the nature of implication is not at the present time clearly defined. And as Jerrold Katz has indicated in his book, *Semantic Theory,* the linguistic judgments that humans are able to make regardless of the particular language they happen to speak are numerous. They can identify semantic redundancy, as in "I saw a naked nude"; contradiction, as in "The sentence I am presently reading is false"; analytic truths or tautologies, as in "Kings are monarchs"; entailment where a sentence like "John is a university professor" would supposedly entail the fact that John can read and write; self-answered questions, like "What is the color of my red tie?"; paraphrase whereby "William hit a policeman" would be judged to have the same truth value as, "Bill slugged a cop"; semantic similarity whereby *aunt, cow, nun, sister, woman, filly,* and *actress* would all be judged the same according to the feature sex which in this case is female; and various types of antonymy whereby *whispered* would be judged as antonymous with *shouted.* People also recognize superordination whereby we know that *a human* is automatically *an animal,* which is automatically *a living thing,* which is automatically *a concrete object,* etc. People also recognize semantic anomaly as in Martin Joos's sentence, "I've never seen a horse smoke a dozen oranges"; semantic ambiguity, as in "Take your pick," and impossible answers, as when "John loves to eat fruit," is judged an inappropriate response to the question, "When did John arrive?"

There are, of course, other universals which may be innate, accidental, or historical in Nature, and it's very difficult to keep these categories separate. However, we have tried to give some insights into the kinds of universals which have a semantic or real-world base. But as we said earlier in this book, the observations and analyses which we have made are by no means definitive or final. This whole area of linguistic research is only in the beginning stages.

Bibliography

Adams, Douglas, *et. al.* (eds.). *Seventh Regional Meeting: Chicago Linguistics Society.* University of Chicago, Department of Linguistics, 1971.

Allen, Robert L. *English Grammars and English Grammar.* New York: Scribner's Sons, 1972.

———. *The Verb System of Present-Day American English.* The Hague: Mouton, 1966; reviewed by Don L. F. Nilsen, 1969.

Alston, William P. "How Does One Tell Whether a Word Has One, Several or Many Senses?" in Steinberg and Jakobovits, 35-47.

Anderson, John. "Adjectives, Datives and Ergativisation," *Foundations of Language,* (August, 1969), 301-23.

———. "The Case for Cause: A Preliminary Enquiry," *Journal of Linguistics,* VI (February, 1970), 99-104.

———. "Ergative and Nominative in English," *Journal of Linguistics,* IV (April, 1968), 1-30.

———. *The Grammar of Case: Towards a Localistic Theory.* Cambridge: Cambridge University Press, 1971.

———. "A Note on 'Rank and Delicacy,' " *Journal of Linguistics,* 1969, 129-35.

———. "On the Status of 'Lexical Formatives,' " *Foundations of Language,* IV (August, 1968), 308-18.

Anderson, Stephen R. "On the Role of Deep Structure in Semantic Interpretation," *Foundations of Language,* VII (August, 1971), 387-96.

Anderson, Wallace L., and Norman C. Stageberg (eds.). *Introductory Readings on Language, Revised Edition*, New York: Holt, Rinehart and Winston, 1966.

Anglin, Jeremy M. *The Growth of Word Meaning*. Cambridge, Mass.: MIT Press, 1970.

Anthony, Edward M. *Toward a Theory of Lexical Meaning: An Essay*. Pittsburgh, Pa., University of Pittsburgh Press, 1973.

Apresyan, Yu D., I. A. Mel'cuk, and A. K. Zolkovsky. "Semantics and Lexicography: Towards a New Type of Unilingual Dictionary," in Keifer, 1969, 1-33.

Austin, John L. "How to Do Things with Words," *The William James Lectures Delivered at Harvard University in 1955*. New York: Oxford University Press, 1962.

Ayer, Alfred Jules. *Language, Truth, and Logic*. New York: Dover Publications, 1952.

Bach, Emmon. *"Have* and *be* in English Syntax," *Language,* LXIII (June, 1967), 462-85.

———. "Nouns and Noun-phrases," in Bach and Harms, 1968, 90-102.

———. "On Some Recurrent Types of Transformations," *Monograph Series on Languages and Linguistics 16th Annual Round Table,* Number 18, Washington, D.C.: Georgetown University Institute of Languages and Linguistics, 1965.

Bach, Emmon, and Robert Harms (eds.). *Universals in Linguistic Theory.* New York: Holt, Rinehart, and Winston, 1968.

Bar-Hillel, Yehoshua. "Dictionaries and Meaning Rules." *Foundations of Language,* III (November, 1967), 409-14.

Beardsley, Monroe C. *Thinking Straight: Principles of Reasoning for Readers and Writers* (2nd ed.). Englewood Cliffs, N.J.: Prentice-Hall, 1956.

Becker, A. L., and D. G. Arms. "Prepositions as Predicates," in Binnick, *et al.,* 1969, 1-11.

Bellert, Irena. "Arguments and Predicates in the Logico-Semantic Structure of Utterances," in Kiefer, 1969, 34-54.

———. "On the Semantic Interpretation of Subject-Predicate Relations in Sentences of Particular Reference," in Bierwisch and Heidolph, 1970, 9-26.

Bendix, Edward, Herman. "Componential Analysis of General Vocabulary: The Semantic Structure of a Set of Verbs in English, Hindi, and Japanese," *International Journal of American Linguistics*, XXII, (April, 1966); reviewed by Charles Fillmore, Part II of Fillmore's review appears in *Working Papers in Linguistics*, Report No. 2, (Computer and Information Science Research Center of Ohio State University, 1968), 30-64.

———. "The Data of Semantic Description," in Steinberg and Jakobovits, 1971, 393-409.

Benjamin, Robert L. *Semantics and Language Analysis.* New York: Bobbs-Merrill, 1970.

Bennett, D.C. "English Prepositions: A Stratificational Approach," *Journal of Linguistics,* IV (October, 1968), 153-72.

Berger, Louis S. "Thoughts on the Semantics of Information," *Etc.,* XXVIII (December, 1971), 421-25.

Berman, Arlene. "Agent, Experiencer and Controllability," *Mathematical Linguistics and Automatic Translation,* Report No. NSF-24 (The Computation Laboratory of Harvard University, (1970), 203-38.

Bever, Thomas G., and Peter S. Rosenbaum. "Some Lexical Structures and Their Empirical Validity," in Steinberg and Jakobovits, 1971, 586-600; reprinted from Jacobs and Rosenbaum, 1970, 3-19.

Bierwisch, Manfred. "On Classifying Semantic Features," in Steinberg and Jakobovits, 1971, 510-35, also in Bierwisch and Heidolph, 1970, 27-50.

Bierwisch, Manfred, and Karl-Heinz Heidolph. *Progress in Linguistics.* The Hague: Mouton, 1970.

Bierwisch, Manfred, and F. Kiefer. "Remarks on Definitions in Natural Language," in Kiefer, 1969, 55-79.

Binkert, Peter J. "Case and Prepositional Constructions in a Transformational Grammar of Classical Latin." Unpublished Ph.D. dissertation, University of Michigan, 1970.

Binnick, Robert. "Ambiguity and Vagueness," in Campbell, *et al.,* 147-53.

———. "On the Nature of the 'Lexical Item,' " in Darden, *et al.,* 1968, 1-13.

Binnick, Robert I., *et al.* (eds.). *Fifth Regional Meeting: Chicago Linguistics Society.* University of Chicago, Department of Linguistics, 1969.

Black, Max, *Models and Metaphors.* Ithaca, N.Y.: Cornell University Press, 1962.

——— "Presuppositions and Implication," in Black, 1962, 48-63.

Blake, Frank. "A Semantic Analysis of Case," in *Curme Volume of Linguistic Studies* (Language Monograph Number 7), edited by J. T. Hartfield and W. Leopold, Baltimore: Waverly Press, 1930, 34-49.

Boas, Franz. "On Geographical Names of the Kwakiutl," in Humes, 1964, 171-81.

Borkin, Ann. "Chipping Away at Meaning," in Peranteau, *et al.,* 1972, 10-21.

Botha, Rudolf P. *The Function of the Lexicon in Transformational Generative Grammar.* The Hague: Mouton, 1968.

Bowers, John. "Adjectives and Adverbs in English." Bloomington, Ind., Indiana University, Linguistics Club, 1970.

Brekle, Herbert E. "Generative Semantics vs. Deep Syntax," in Kiefer, 1969, 80-90.

Campbell, Mary Ann, *et al.,* (eds.). *Sixth Regional Meeting: Chicago Linguistics Society,* University of Chicago, Department of Linguistics, 1970.

Carnap, Rudolf. "Foundations of Logic and Mathematics," in Fodor and Katz, 1964, pp. 419-36; reprinted from *International Encyclopedia of Unified Science,* 1, 143-71.

Carroll, John B. *Language and Thought.* New York: Prentice-Hall, 1964.

———. *Language, Thought, and Reality: Selected Writings of Benjamin Lee Whorf.* Cambridge, Mass.: MIT Press, 1956.

Cassidy, F. G. " 'Case' in Modern English," in *Language,* XIII (July-September 1937), 240-45.

Caton, Charles E. "Philosophy: Overview," in Steinberg and Jakobovits, 1971, 3-13.

Chafe, Wallace L. "Linguistics and Human Knowledge," *Monograph Series on Languages and Linguistics, 22nd Annual Round Table,* Number 24, Washington, D.C.: Georgetown University Institute of Languages and Linguistics, 1971.

———. *Meaning and the Structure of Language.* Chicago: University of Chicago Press, 1970; reviewed by Don L. F. Nilsen, 1971; also reviewed by Frank W. Heny, 1972.

Chapin, Paul. "On the Syntax of Word-Derivation in English." Bedford, Mass., The MITRE Corporation, 1967.

Chomsky, Noam. *Aspects of the Theory of Syntax.* Cambridge, Mass.: MIT Press, 1965; reviewed by P. H. Matthews, 1967.

———. "Current Issues in Linguistic Theory," in Fodor and Katz, 1964, 50-118.

———. "Deep Structure, Surface Structure and Semantic Interpretation," in Steinberg and Jakobovits, 1971, pp. 183-216; also in Jakobson, 1970, 52-91.

———. "Degrees of Grammaticalness," in Fodor and Katz, 1964, 384-89; reprinted from "Some Methodological Remarks on Generative Grammar," *Word,* XVII (August, 1961), 219-39.

———. "Generative Grammars As Theories of Linguistic Competence," in Reibel and Schane, 1969, 13-18.

———. *Language and Mind* (enlarged edition). New York: Harcourt, Brace and World, 1972.

———. "Remarks on Nominalization." Bloomington, Ind., Indiana University Linguistics Club, 1968; also in Jacobs and Rosenbaum, 1968, 184-221.

———. *Studies on Semantics in Generative Grammar.* The Hague: Mouton, 1972.

———. *Syntactic Structures.* The Hague: Mouton, 1957.

———. "Topics in the Theory of Generative Grammar," in Sebeok, 1966, 1-60.

———. "A Transformational Approach to Syntax," in *Proceedings of the Third Texas Conference on Problems of Linguistic Analysis in English,* edited by Archibald Hill, Austin, Texas: University of Texas Press, 1962.

Church, Alonzo. "The Need for Abstract Entities in Semantic Analysis," in Fodor and Katz, 437-45; reprinted from *Contributions to the Analysis and Synthesis of Knowledge, Proceedings of the American Academy of Arts and Sciences*, LXXX (July, 1951), 100-12.

Conklin, Harold C. "Hanuoo Color Categories," in Hymes, 1964, 189-92.

Dale, Philip S. *Language Development: Structure and Function.* Hinsdale, Ill.: The Dryden Press, 1972.

Darden, Bill J., *et al.* (eds.). *Fourth Regional Meeting: Chicago Linguistics Society. University of Chicago, Department of Linguistics, 1968.*

Davis, Philip W. *Modern Theories of Language.* Englewood Cliffs, N.J.: Prentice-Hall, 1973.

Davis, Steven, "Meaning and the Transformational Stew," *Foundations of Language,* VI (February, 1970), 67-88.

Davison, Alice. "Causal Adverbs and Performative Verbs," in Campbell, *et al.,* 190-201.

De Groot, A. Willem. "Classification of Cases and Uses of Cases," in *For Roman Jakobson,* edited by Morris Halle, The Hague: Mouton, 1956.

Devito, Joseph A. *General Semantics: Guide and Workbook.* Deland, Fla.: Everett/Edwards, 1971.

Dixon, R. M. W. "A Method of Semantic Description," in Steinberg and Jakobovits, 1971, 436-71.

―――. "Syntactic Orientation as a Semantic Property," *Mathematical Linguistics and Automatic Translation,* Report No. NSF-24 (The Computation Laboratory of Harvard University, 1970), 1-22

Dolliver, Robert H., and Wayne P. Anderson. "Polarities, Perceptions, and Problems," *Etc.,* XXVIII (September, 1971), 293-301.

Donnellan, Keith. "References and Definite Descriptions," in Steinberg and Jakobovits, 1971, pp. 100-14; reprinted from *Philosophical Review,* LXXV (July, 1966), 281-304.

Dowty, David R. "On the Syntax and Semantics of the Atomic Predicate *Cause,*" in Peranteau, *et al.,* 1972, 62-74.

Dressler, Wolfgang. "Towards a Semantic Deep Structure of Discourse Grammar," in Campbell, *et al.,* 1970, 202-209.

Dupraz, M., and J. Rousault. "Lexis―Affirmation―Négation: Etude Fondée sur les Classes," in Kiefer, 1969, 91-108.

Elliot, Dale. "The Grammar of Emotive and Exclamatory Sentences in English," *Working Papers in Linguistics,* Report No. 8, (Computer and Information Science Research Center of Ohio State University, 1970), viii-110.

Emonds, Joseph. "Constraints on Transformations." Bloomington, Ind., Indiana University Linguistics Club, 1969.

Fillmore, Charles J. "The Case for Case," in Bach and Harms, 1968, 1-90.

———. "Deictic Categories in the Semantics of 'Come,'" *Foundations of Language,* II (August, 1966), 219-27.

———. "Entailment Rules in a Semantic Theory," *Project on Linguistic Analysis,* Report No. 10, (Ohio State University, 1965), 60-82.

———. "On Generativity," *Working Papers in Linguistics,* Report No. 6 (Computer and Information Science Research Center of Ohio State University, 1970), 1-19.

———. "The Grammar of Hitting and Breaking," *Project on Linguistic Analysis,* Report Number 1 (Ohio State University, 1967), 9-29; also in Jacobs and Rosenbaum, 1968, 120-33.

———. *Indirect Object Constructions in English and the Ordering of Transformations.* The Hague: Mouton, 1965; reviewed by Don L. F. Nilsen, 1968.

———. "Lexical Entries for Verbs," *Foundations of Language,* IV (November, 1968), 373-93; also in *Working Papers in Linguistics,* Report No. 2, (Computer and Information Science Research Center of Ohio State University, 1968), 1-29.

———. "On the Notion of 'Equivalent Sentence Structure,'" *Project on Linguistic Analysis,* Report Number 11 (Ohio State University, 1965), 118-28.

———. "The Position of Embedding Transformations in a Grammar," *Word,* XIX, (August, 1963), 208-31.

———. "Some Problems for Case Grammar," *Working Papers in Linguistics,* Report Number 10, (Computer and Information Science Research Center of Ohio State University, 1971), 245-265; originally presented at the 1971 Georgetown Roundtable on Linguistics, at Georgetown University on March 11, 1971, Number 24, 35-36.

———. "A Proposal Concerning English Prepositions," *Monograph Series on Languages and Linguistics 17th Annual Round Table,* Number 19, Washington, D.C.: Georgetown University Institute of Languages and Linguistics, 1966.

———. Review of "Componential Analysis of General Vocabulary: The Semantic Structure of a Set of Verbs in English, Hindi, and Japanese," by Edward Herman Bendix, in *General Linguistics,* IX (1969), 41-65.

———. "Subjects, Speakers and Roles," *Working Papers in Linguistics,* Report No. 4, Columbus, Ohio: The Ohio State University (Computer and Information Science Research Center of Ohio State University, 1970), 31-63.

———. "On the Syntax of Preverbs," *Glossa,* I (1967), 91-125.

———. "Toward a Modern Theory of Case," *Project on Linguistic Analysis,* Report No. 13 (Ohio State University, 1966), 1-24; also in Reibel and Schane, 1969, 316-76.

———. "Types of Lexical Information," in Kiefer, 1969, 109-37; also in *Proceedings of the Balatonszabadi Conference of Mathematical Linguistics*, edited by Ferenc Kiefer (Reidel); also in *Working Papers in Linguistics*, Report No. 2, (Computer and Information Science Research Center of Ohio State University, 1968), 65-103; also in Steinberg and Jakobovits, 1971, 370-92.

———. "Verbs of Judging: An Exercise in Semantic Description," in Fillmore and Langendoen, 1971, 272-89.

Fillmore, Charles J., and D. Terence Langendoen (eds.). *Studies in Linguistic Semantics.* New York: Holt, Rinehart and Winston, 1971.

Finne, W. Bruce, and Thomas Erskine (eds.). *Words on Words: A Language Reader.* New York: Random House, 1971.

Fodor, Jerry A. "Could Meaning be an r_m?" in Steinberg and Jakobovits, 1971, pp. 558-68; reprinted from *Journal of Verbal Learning and Verbal Behavior,* IV (April, 1965), 73-81.

———. "Three Reasons for Not Deriving 'Kill' from 'Cause to Die,' " *Linguistic Inquiry,* I (October, 1970), 429-38.

Fodor, Jerry, and Jerrold J. Katz (eds.). *The Structure of Language: Readings in the Philosophy of Language.* Englewood Cliffs, N.J.: Prentice-Hall, 1964.

Frake, Charles O. "The Diagnosis of Disease Among the Subanun of Mindanao," in Hymes, 1964, 193-211.

Fraser, Bruce. "An Analysis of Concessive Conditionals," in Binnick, *et al.,* 1969, 66-75.

———. "An Analysis of 'Even' in English," in Fillmore and Langendoen, 1971, 150-178.

———. "An Examination of Verb-Particle Constructions in English." Unpublished Ph.D. dissertation, MIT, 1965.

———. "Idioms within a Transformational Grammar," *Foundations of Language,* VI (February, 1970), 22-42.

———. "Some Remarks on the Action Nominalization in English" in Jacobs and Rosenbaum, 1970, 83-98.

———. "Some Remarks on the Verb-Particle Construction in English," *Monograph Series on Languages and Linguistics, 17th Annual Round Table,* Number 19, Washington, D.C.: Georgetown University Institute of Languages and Linguistics, 1966.

Friedman, Joyce. "Lexical Insertion, N-ary Features and Case Grammars." Unpublished paper, University of Michigan, 1970.

Fromkin, Victoria, and Robert Rodman. *An Introduction to Language.* New York: Holt, Rinehart, and Winston, 1974.

Garner, Richard. "Presupposition in Philosophy and Linguistics," in Fillmore and Langendoen, 1971, 22-42.

Geis, Michael and Arnold Zwicky. "On Invited Inferences," *Working Papers in Linguistics*, Report No. 8, (Computer and Information Science Research Center of Ohio State University, 1971), 150-55.

Gleitman, Lila. "Coordinating Conjunctions in English," *Language,* XLI (April-June, 1965), 260-93; reprinted in Reibel and Schane, 1969, 80-112.

Goodenough, Ward H. "Language and Property in Truk: Some Methodological Considerations," in Hymes, 1964, 185-88.

Goodman, Ralph M. "A Generative Propositional Grammar." Unpublished Ph.D. dissertation, UCLA, 1970.

–––. *A History of Transformational Grammar.* New York: Holt, Rinehart and Winston, to appear.

Gordon, David, and George Lakoff. "Conversational Postulates," Adams *et al.,* 1971, 63-84.

Green, Georgia. "On *too* and *either,* and Not Just on *too* and *either,* Either," in Darden, *et al.,* 1968, 22-39.

–––. "On the Notion 'Related Lexical Entry,' " in Binnick, *et al.,* 1969, 76-88.

–––. "Some Observations on the Syntax and Semantics of Instrumental Verbs," in Peranteau, *et al.* 1972, 83-97.

Greenberg, Joseph H. (ed.). *Universals of Language* (2nd ed.). Cambridge, Mass.: MIT Press, 1966.

Greene, Judith. *Psycholinguistics, Chomsky and Psychology.* New York: Penguin, 1972.

Grice, H. P. "Meaning," in Steinberg and Jakobovits, 1971, pp. 53-59; reprinted from *Philosophical Review,* LXVI (July, 1957), 377-88.

–––. "Utterer's Meaning, Sentence-Meaning, and Word Meaning," *Foundations of Language,* IV (August, 1968), 225-42.

Grinder, John T., and Suzette Haden Elgin, *Guide to Transformational Grammar: History, Theory, Practice.* New York: Holt, Rinehart and Winston, 1973.

Grosu, Alexander, "On Perceptual and Grammatical Constraints," *Working Papers in Linguistics*, Report No. 8, (Computer and Information Science Research Center of Ohio State University, 1971), 136-49.

Gruber, Jeffrey S. "Topicalization in Child Language," in Reibel and Schane, 1969, 422-47.

Hale, Austin. "Conditions on English Comparative Clause Pairings," in Jacobs and Rosenbaum, 1970, 30-55.

Hale, Kenneth. "A Note on a Walbiri Tradition of Antonymy," in Steinberg and Jakobovits, 1971, 472-84.

Halliday, M. A. K. "Notes on Transitivity and Theme in English," *Journal of Linguistics*, III (April, 1968), 37-81, IV (October, 1969), 179-216.

Harman, Gilbert H. "Three Levels of Meaning," in Steinberg and Jakobovits, 1971, 66-75; reprinted from *The Journal of Philosophy*, LXV (October, 1968), 590-602.

Harris, Zellig S. "Discourse Analysis," in Fodor and Katz, 1964, 335-83.

Hasegawa, Kinsuke. "Transformations and Semantic Interpretation," *Linguistic Inquiry*, III (Spring, 1972), 141-59.

Hayakawa, S. I. *Language in Thought and Action* (3rd ed.). New York: Harcourt, Brace Jovanovich, 1972.

Hays, David G. "Linguistic Problems of Denotation," in Bierwisch and Heidolph, 1970, 81-85.

Heny, Frank W. "Review of *Meaning and the Structure of Language*" by Wallace L. Chafe, in *College English*, XIII, (May, 1972), 908-29.

Heringer, James Tromp, Jr. "Some Grammatical Correlates of Felicty Conditions and Presuppositions," *Working Papers in Linguistics*, Report No. 11, (Computer and Information Science Research Center of Ohio State University, 1972), 1-110.

Hetzron, Robert. "The Deep Structure of the Statement," *Linguistics*, LXV (January, 1971), 25-63.

Horn, Larry. "A Presuppositional Analysis of 'Only' and 'Even,' " in Binnick, *et al.*, 1969, 98-107.

Householder, Fred W., and Sol Saporta. *Problems in Lexicography*. The Hague: Mouton, 1967.

Huddleston, Rodney D. "Some Remarks on Case Grammar," *Linguistic Inquiry*, I (October, 1970), 501-11.

Hutchins, W. J. *The Generation of Syntactic Structure from a Semantic Base*. Amsterdam: North-Holland Publishing Company, 1971.

Hutchinson, Larry G. "Presupposition and Belief-inferences," in Adams *et al.*, 134-41.

Hymes, Dell (ed.). *Language in Culture and Society*. New York: Harper and Row, 1964.

―――. "Cultural Focus and Semantic Field: Introduction," in Hymes, 1964, 165-70.

Ingram, David. "Transitivity in Child Language," *Language*, XLVII (December, 1971), 888-910.

Jackendoff, Ray S. *Semantic Interpretation in Generative Grammar*. Cambridge, Mass.: MIT Press, 1972.

―――. "Some Rules for English Semantic Interpretation." Unpublished Ph.D. dissertation, MIT, 1969.

―――. "Model Structure in Semantic Representation," *Linguistic Inquiry*, II, (Fall, 1971), 479-514.

Jacobs, Roderick A., and Peter S. Rosenbaum. *English Transformational Grammar*. Waltham, Mass.: Blaisdell, 1968; reviewed by Don F. Nilsen, 1970.

———. (eds.). *Readings in English Transformational Grammar.* Waltham, Mass.: Blaisdell, 1970.

———. *Transformations, Style, and Meaning.* Waltham, Mass.: Xerox College Publishing, 1971.

Jacobson, Roman (ed.). *Studies in Oriental and General Linguistics.* Tokyo: TEC Corporation for Language and Educational Research, 1970.

James, Deborah. "Some Aspects of The Syntax and Semantics of Interjections," in Peranteau, *et al.*, 1972, 162-72.

Johnson, Valdon L. "Conditions of a Private Language." Paper read at the University of Iowa, Summer, 1972.

Joos, Martin (ed.). *Readings in Linguistics.* New York: American Council of Learned Societies, 1958.

———. "Semantic Axiom Number One," *Language,* XLVIII (June, 1972), 257-65.

Karltuven, Lanni. "Possible and Must," in Kimball, 1973, 1-20.

Katz, Jerrold J. "Analyticity and Contradiction in Natural Language," in Fodor and Katz, 519-43.

———. "Generative Semantics is Interpretive Semantics," *Linguistic Inquiry,* II (Summer, 1971), 313-31.

———. "Interpretative Semantics vs. Generative Semantics," *Foundations of Language,* VI (May, 1970) 220-59.

———. *The Philosophy of Language.* New York: Harper and Row, 1966.

———. "Recent Issues in Semantic Theory," *Foundations of Language,* III (May, 1967), 124-94.

———. *Semantic Theory.* New York: Harper and Row, 1972.

———. "Semantic Theory," in Steinberg and Jakobovits, 1971, 297-307; reprinted from Katz, 1966, 151-75.

———. "Semi-sentences," in Fodor and Katz, 1964, 400-16.

Katz, Jerrold J., and Paul M. Postal. *An Integrated Theory of Linguistic Descriptions,* Cambridge, Mass.: MIT Press, 1964.

Kay, Martin. "From Semantics to Syntax," in Bierwisch and Heidolph, 1970, 114-26.

Kay, Paul. "Taxonomy and Semantic Contrast," *Language,* XLVII (December, 1971), 866-87.

Keenan, Edward L. "Two Kinds of Presupposition in Natural Language," in Fillmore and Langendoen, 1971, 44-52.

Kernan, Keith T. "Semantic Relationships and the Child's Acquisition of Language," *Anthropological Linguistics,* XII (May, 1970), 171-87.

Kiefer, Ferenc. *Mathematical Linguistics in Eastern Europe.* New York: Elsevier Publishing Company, 1968.

———. (ed.). *Studies in Syntax and Semantics.* Dordrecht, Holland: Reidel, 1969.

Kimball, John P. (ed.). *Syntax and Semantics* (2 vols.). New York: Seminar Press, 1973.

King, David, and Thomas Crerar. *A Choice of Words.* Toronto: Oxford University Press, 1969.

Kiparsky, Paul, and Carol Kiparsky. "Fact," in Bierwisch and Heidolph, 1970, 143-73; also in Steinberg and Jakobovits, 1971, 345-69.

Klima, Edward S. "Negation in English," in Fodor and Katz, 1964, 246-323.

Kooij, Jan G. *Ambiguity in Natural Language: An Investigation of Certain Problems in Its Linguistic Description.* Amsterdam: North-Holland Publishing Company, 1971; reviewed by Don L. F. Nilsen, (1973).

Korzybski, Alfred. *Science and Sanity.* New York: Institute of General Semantics, 1958.

Kuno, Susumo. "Some Properties of Nonreferential Noun Phrases," in Jakobson, 1970.

Kuroda, S. Y. "Remarks on Selectional Restrictions and Presuppositions," in Kiefer, 1969, 138-67.

———. "Some Remarks on Adverbs," *The English Record,* XX (April, 1970), 69-78.

Lakoff, George. "Deep Surface Grammar." Bloomington, Ind.: Indiana University Linguistics Club, 1968.

———. "Hedges: A Study of Meaning Criteria and the Logic of Fuzzy Concepts," in Peranteau, *et al.,* 1972, 183-228.

———. "On Derivational Constraints," in Binnick, *et al.,* 1969, 117-39.

———. "On Generative Semantics," in Steinberg and Jakobovits, 1971, 232-96.

———. "Instrumental Adverbs and the Concept of Deep Structure," *Foundations of Language,* IV (February, 1968), 4-29.

———. *Irregularity in Syntax.* New York: Holt, Rinehart and Winston, 1970.

———. "Linguistics and Natural Logic," in *Studies in Generative Semantics I,* Ann Arbor, University of Michigan Phonetics Laboratory, 1970.

———. "Natural Logic and Lexical Decomposition," in Campbell, *et al.,* 1970, 340-62.

———. "On the Nature of Syntactic Irregularity," *Mathematical Linguistics and Automatic Translation,* Report No. NSF-16 (The Computation Laboratory of Harvard University; 1965), i-xiii and O-1 to R-27.

———. "Presuppositions and Relative Well-formedness," in Steinberg and Jakobovits, 1971, 329-40.

———. "Pronominalization, Negation, and the Analysis of Adverbs." Mimeographed, Harvard University, 1967; also in Jacobs and Rosenbaum, 1970, 145-165.

———. "Repartee, or a Reply to 'Negation, Conjunction and Quantifiers,' " *Foundations of Language,* VI (August, 1970), 389-422.

———. "The Role of Deduction in Grammar," in Fillmore and Langendoen, 1971, 62-70.

———. "Stative Adjectives and Verbs in English," in Harvard Computational

Laboratory Report NSF-17, edited by Anthony G. Oettinger, *et al.* (August, 1966), I-1 to I-16.

Lakoff, George, and John Robert Ross. "A Criterion for Verb Phrase Constituency," *Mathematical Linguistics and Automatic Translation*, Report No. NSF-17 (the Computational Laboratory of Harvard University, 1966), II-1 to II-11.

Lakoff, George, and Stanley Peters. "Phrasal Conjunction and Symmetric Predicates," in Reibel and Schane, 1969, pp. 113-42; reprinted from NSF-17 (1967), 80-112.

Lakoff, Robin. "If's, And's, and But's about Conjunction," in Fillmore and Langendoen, 1971, 114-49.

———. "A Syntactic Argument for Negative Transportation," in Binnick, *et al.*, 1969, 140-47.

Lambert, Dorothy Mack. "The Semantic Syntax of Metaphor: A Case Grammar Analysis." Unpublished Ph.D. dissertation, University of Michigan (Ann Arbor), 1969.

Lamberts, J. J. *A Short Introduction to English Usage.* New York: McGraw-Hill, 1972.

Lamendella, John T. "Long-Term Memory, Conceptual Structure and a Theory of Generative Semantics." Unpublished Ph.D. dissertation, University of Michigan, 1969.

Langacker, Ronald W. *Language and its Structure,* (2nd ed.). New York: Harcourt Brace Jovanovich, 1973.

———. "Pronominalization and the Chain of Command," in Reibel and Schane, 1969, 160-86.

Langendoen, D. Terence. "The Accessibility of Deep Structures," in Jacobs and Rosenbaum, 99-104.

———. *Essentials of English Grammar.* New York: Holt, Rinehart and Winston, 1970.

———. "Presupposition and Assertion in the Semantic Analysis of Nouns and Verbs in English," in Steinberg and Jakobovits, 1971, 341-44.

———. *The Study of Syntax.* New York: Holt, Rinehart and Winston, 1969.

Langendoen, D. Terence, and Harris B. Savin. "The Projection Problem for Presuppositions," in Fillmore and Langendoen, 1971, 45-60.

Langer, Susanne. *Philosophy in a New Key.* New York: New American Library, 1948.

Lee, P. Gregory. "The English Preposition *With,* " *Working Papers in Linguistics*, Report No. 1, (Computer and Information Science Research Center of Ohio State University, 1967), 31-79.

———. "Notes in Defense of Case Grammar," in Adams *et al.*, 1971, 174-80.

———. "Subjects and Agents," *Working Papers in Linguistics*, Report No. 3, (Computer and Information Science Research Center of Ohio State University, 1970), 30-79; "Subjects and Agents Part II," *Working Papers in Linguistics*, Report No. 7, (Computer and Information Science Research Center, 1971), i-iii and L-1 to L-118.

Lee, Patricia. "A Note on Manner Adverbs," *Working Papers in Linguistics*, Report No. 4, (Computer and Information Science Research Center, 1970), 74-84.

Leech, Geoffrey, N. *Meaning and the English Verb*. London: Longman, 1971.

———. *Towards a Semantic Description of English*. Bloomington, Ind.: Indiana University Press, 1970.

Lees, Robert B. "A Multiply Ambiguous Adjectival Construction in English," *Language*, XXXVI (April-June, 1962), 207-21.

———. "On Very Deep Grammatical Structure," in Jacobs and Rosenbaum, 1970, 134-44.

———. "Two Views of Linguistics Research," *Linguistics*, XI (January, 1965), 21-29.

Legum, Stanley E. "The Verb-Particle Construction in English, Basic or Derived," in Darden, *et al.*, 1968, 50-62.

Lehrer, Adrienne. "Verbs and Deletable Objects," *Lingua*, XXV (August, 1970), 227-53.

Lekawatana, Pongeri. "Verb Phrases in Thai: A Study in Deep-Case Relationships." Unpublished Ph.D. dissertation, University of Michigan, 1970.

Lenneberg, Eric H. "Language and Cognition," in Steinberg and Jakobovits, 1971, 536-57; a revision of Chapter 8 ("Language and Cognition") of *Biological Foundations of Language* by Eric Lenneberg, New York: John Wiley and Sons, 1967.

Lester, Mark (ed.). *Readings in Applied Transformational Grammar*. New York: Holt, Rinehart and Winston, 1970.

Liles, Bruce L. *Linguistics and the English Language, A Transformational Approach*. Pacific Palisades, Calif: Goodyear Publishing Company, 1972.

Lin, Nan. *The Study of Human Communication*. New York: Bobbs-Merrill, 1973.

Lindholm, James M. "Negative-Raising and Sentence Pronominalization," in Binnick, *et al.*, 1969, 148-58.

Linsky, Leonard. "Reference and Referents," in Steinberg and Jakobovits, 1971, 76-85; Chapter 8 in *Referring* by Leonard Linsky, New York: Humanities Press, 1967.

Lipka, Leonhard. *Semantic Structure and Word Formation*. München-Wilhelm Press, 1967.

Locke, William N., and A. Donald Booth (eds.). *Machine Translation of Languages.* Cambridge, Mass.: MIT Press, 1955.

Lotz, John. "On Language and Culture," in Hymes, 1964, 182-84.

Lu, John H. T. "Contrastive Stress and Emphatic Stress," *Project on Linguistic Analysis,* Report Number 10 (May, 1965), Ohio State University, 38-59.

Luce, Duncan, Robert R. Bush, and Eugene Galanter (eds.). *Handbook of Mathematical Psychology,* (vol. II). New York: John Wiley and Sons, 1963.

Lyons, John. *Introduction to Theoretical Linguistics.* Cambridge: Cambridge University Press, 1969.

———. "A Note on Possessive, Existential, and Locative Sentences," *Foundations of Language,* III (November, 1967), 390-96.

———. *Noam Chomsky.* New York: Viking, 1970.

———. "Towards a 'Notional' Theory of the 'Parts of Speech,'" *Journal of Linguistics,* II (October, 1966), 209-36.

McCawley, James, D. "Concerning the Base Component of a Transformational Grammar," *Foundations of Language,* IV (August, 1968), 243-69.

———. "English as a VSO Language," *Language,* XLVI (June, 1970), 286-99.

———. "Lexical Insertion in a Transformational Grammar without Deep Structure," in Darden, *et al.,* 1968, 71-80.

———. "Meaning and the Description of Language," *Kotoba No Uchu,* II, Nos. 9-11 (1967).

———. "The Role of Semantics in Grammar," in Bach and Harms, 1968, 125-69.

———. "Tense and Time Reference in English," in Fillmore and Langendoen, 1971, 96-113.

———. "Where Do Noun Phrases Come From?" in Jacobs and Rosenbaum, 1970, 166-83; also in Steinberg and Jakobovits, 1971, 217-31.

McCoy, Ana Maria Bartrina Compos. "A Case Grammar Classification of Spanish Verbs." Unpublished Ph.D. dissertation, University of Michigan, 1969.

Maclay, Howard. "Linguistics: Overview," in Steinberg and Jakobovits, 1971, 157-82.

McNeill, David. "Are There Specifically Linguistic Universals?" in Steinberg and Jakobovits, 1971, 530-35.

Marino, Mathew. "The Role of Lexicon in a Case Grammar." Unpublished Ph.D. dissertation, University of Michigan, 1970.

Matthews, P. H. "Review of *Aspects of the Theory of Syntax,*" by Noam Chomsky, in *Journal of Linguistics,* III (April, 1967), 119-52.

Matthews, Robert J. "Concerning a 'Linguistic Theory' of Metaphor," *Foundations of Language,* VII (August, 1971), 411-25.

Messing, Gordon M. "The Impact of Transformational Grammar upon Stylistics and Literary Analysis," *Linguistics,* LXVI (February, 1971), 56-73.

Miller, D. Gary. "Cases as Underlying Verbs." Unpublished paper, University of Illinois, 1970.

Miller, George A. "Empirical Methods in the Study of Semantics," in Steinberg and Jakobovits, 1971, 569-85; Part of II, *Psycholinguistic Approaches to the Study of Communication*, in *Journeys in Science: Small Steps–Great Strides*, edited by D. L. Arm, Albuquerque, University of New Mexico Press, 1967.

Minteer, Catherine. *Words and What They Do to You.* New York: Row Peterson, 1952.

Miron, Murray S. "The Semantic Differential and Mediation Theory," *Linguistics,* LXVI (February, 1971), 74-87.

Morgan, Jerry. "Remarks on the Notion 'Possible Lexical Item.' " Unpublished paper, University of Chicago, 1968.

———. "On the Treatment of Presuppositions in Transformational Grammar," in Binnick, *et al.,* 1969, 169-77.

Morin, Yves Ch. "A Second Order Case Grammar." Unpublished paper, University of Michigan, 1969.

Morin, Yves Ch., and Michael H. O'Malley. "Multi-Rooted Vines in Semantic Representation," in Binnick, *et al.,* 1969, 178-85.

Morris, Charles. *Signification and Significance: A Study of the Relations of Signs and Values.* Cambridge: MIT Press, 1964.

Morley, Roy A., Jr. "Information and the Reduction of Disorder," *Etc.,* XXVIII, (September, 1971), 302-10.

Newmeyer, Frederick J. "On the Alleged Boundary Between Syntax and Semantics," *Foundations of Language,* VI (May, 1970), 178-86.

Nilsen, Don. L. F. *English Adverbials.* The Hague: Mouton, 1972.

———. "English Infinitives," *The Canadian Journal of Linguistics,* XIII (Spring, 1968), 83-93.

———. "The Expletive 'There' from a Transformation Point of View," *Glossa,* III (1969), 101-107.

———. *The Instrumental Case in English: Semantic and Syntactic Considerations.* The Hague: Mouton, 1973.

———. "Lexical Decomposition and the Teaching of Vocabulary," *TEFL Reporter* (Fall, 1972), 13-15.

———. "A Linguistic Analysis of Humor," *The English Record,* XX (February, 1970), 41-56.

———. (ed.). *Meaning–A Common Ground of Linguistics and Literature.* The Hague: Mouton, to appear.

———. "Review of *Ambiguity in Natural Language: An Investigation of Certain Problems in Its Linguistic Description.*" by J.G. Kooij, in *Foundations of Language,* X (1973), 595-97.

———. "Review of *Readings in English Transformational Grammar,*" by Roderick A. Jacobs and Peter S. Rosenbaum, in *Linguistics,* LIX (July, 1970), 113-22.

———. "Review of *Indirect Object Constructions in English and the Ordering of Transformations,*" by Charles J. Fillmore, in *Linguistics,* XLV (1968), 36-43.

———. "Review of *Meaning and the Structure of Language,*" by Wallace L. Chafe, *Lingua,* XXVIII (1971), 124-31.

———. "Review of *The Verb System of Present-Day American English,*" by Robert L. Allen, in *Linguistics,* L, (July, 1969), 112-19.

———. "Some Notes on Case Grammar in English," *Word,* XXVI (August, 1970), 271-77.

———. *Toward a Semantic Specification of Deep Case.* The Hague: Mouton, 1972.

———. "The Use of Case Grammar in Teaching English as a Foreign Language," *TESOL Quarterly,* V (December, 1971), 293-99.

Nobel, Barry. "Evidence" *Working Papers in Linguistics,* Report No. 8 (Computer and Information Science Research Center of Ohio State University, 1971), 164-72.

Ogden, C. K., and I. A. Richards. *The Meaning of Meaning.* New York: Harcourt, Brace and World, 1946.

Osgood, Charles E. "Commentary on 'Semantic Differential and Mediation Theory,'" *Linguistics,* LXVI (February, 1971), 88-96.

———. "Where do Sentences Come From?", in Steinberg and Jakobovits, 1971, pp. 497-529.

Osgood, Charles E., George J. Suci, and Percy H. Tannenbaum. *The Measurement of Meaning.* Urbana, Ill.: University of Illinois Press, 1957.

Paduceva, E. V. "Anaphoric Relations and Their Representation in the Deep Structure of a Text," in Bierwisch and Heidolph, 1970, 224-32.

Pam, Martin D. "The Case for Cash," *Working Papers in Linguistics,* Report No. 10, (Computer and Information Science Research Center of Ohio State University, 1971), 172-81.

Partee, Barbara H. "Negation, Conjunction and Quantifiers: Syntax vs Semantics," *Foundations of Language,* VI (May, 1970, 153-65.

———. "On the Requirement That Transformations Preserve Meaning," in Fillmore and Langendoen, 1971, 1-21.

———. "Subject and Object in English." Unpublished Ph.D. dissertation, MIT, 1965.

Pence, James Monroe. "Implications of Fillmore's Case Grammar for Language Instruction." Unpublished paper, Kabul University, Afghanistan, 1969.

———. "Vocabulary Categories in English Language Instruction." Unpublished paper, Kabul University, Afghanistan, 1969.

Peranteau, Paul, *et al.* (eds.). *Eighth Regional Meeting: Chicago Linguistics Society.* University of Chicago, Department of Linguistics, 1972.

Perlmutter, D. M. "Evidence for Deep Structure Constraints in Syntax," in Kiefer, 1969, 168-86.

———. "The Two Verbs Begin," in Jacobs and Rosenbaum, 1970, pp. 107-19.

Perlmutter, David, and John R. Ross. "Relative Clauses with Split Antecedents," *Linguistic Inquiry,* I (July, 1970), 350.

Petofi, Janos. "On the Structural Analysis and Typology of Poetic Images," in Kiefer, 1969, 187-230.

Postal, Paul M. "Anaphoric Islands," in Binnick, *et al.,* 1969, 205-39.

–––. "Constituent Structure: A Study of Contemporary Models of Syntactic Description," *International Journal of American Linguistics,* XXX (January, 1964), 1-122.

–––. "On Coreferential Complement Subject Deletion," *Linguistic Inquiry,* I (October, 1970), 439-500.

–––. "Limitations on Phrase Structure Grammars," in Fodor and Katz, 1964, 137-51.

–––. "On the So-called Pronouns in English," in Jacobs and Rosenbaum, 1970, 56-82.

–––. "On the Surface Verb 'Remind,' " in Fillmore and Langendoen, 1971, 180-270; reprinted from *Linguistic Inquiry*, I (January, 1970), 37-120.

–––. "Underlying and Superficial Linguistic Structure," *Harvard Educational Review,* XXXIV (Spring, 1964), 246-66; also in Schane, 1969, 19-37.

Quine, W. V. "The Inscrutability of Reference," in Steinberg and Jakobovits, 1971, 142-56; part of Ontological Relativity," in *The Journal of Philosophy,* LXV (April, 1968), 185-212.

–––. *From a Logical Point of View.* (2nd ed., revised). New York: Harper and Row, 1961.

–––. *Mathematical Logic.* New York: Harper and Row, 1951.

–––. "Meaning and Translation," in Fodor and Katz, 1964, 460-78; reprinted from *On Translation*, edited by R. A. Brower (Cambridge, Mass.: Harvard University Press, 1959).

–––. "The Problem of Meaning in Linguistics," in Fodor and Katz, 1964, 21-32.

–––. "Speaking of Objects," in Fodor and Katz, 1964, 446-59; reprinted from *Proceedings and Addresses of the American Philosophical Association 1957-58,* Ohio: Antioch Press, 1958, 5-22.

–––. *Word and Object.* Cambridge, Mass.: MIT Press, 1960.

Raisbeck, Gordon. *Information Theory: An Introduction for Scientists and Engineers.* Cambridge, Mass.: MIT Press, 1963.

Reddy, Michael J. "A Semantic Approach to Metaphor," in Binnick, *et al.,* 1969, 240-51.

Reibel, David, and Sanford Schane (eds.). *Modern Studies in English: Readings in Transformational Grammar.* Englewood Cliffs, N.J.: Prentice-Hall, 1969.

Richards, I. A. *Speculative Instruments.* New York: Harcourt, Brace & World, 1955.

Robinson, Jane J. "Case, Category, and Configuration," *Journal of Linguistics,* VI (February, 1970), 57-60.

Rogers, Andy. "Three Kinds of Physical Perception Verbs," in Adams *et al.,* 206-22.

Rosenbaum, Peter. *The Grammar of English Predicate Complement Construc-tions.* Cambridge, Mass.: MIT Press, 1967; also, *Research Monograph Number 47,* Cambridge, Mass.: MIT Press, 1967.

———. "Phrase Structure Principles of English Complex Sentence Formation," *Journal of Linguistics,* III (April, 1967), 103-18.

———. "A Principal Governing Deletion in English Sentential Complementation," in Jacobs and Rosenbaum, 1970, 20-29.

Rosenbaum, P., and D. Lochak. "The IBM Core Grammar of English," in *Specification and Utilization of a Transformational Grammar,* edited by D. Lieberman, Yorktown Heights, N.Y.: IBM Corporation, 1966, 1-167.

Ross, John R. "Adjectives as Noun Phrases," in Reibel and Schane, 1969, 352-60.

———. *Constraints on Variables in Syntax.* Unpublished Ph.D. dissertation, MIT, 1967; also Bloomington, Ind., Indiana University Linguistics Club, 1968.

———. "On Declarative Sentences," in Jacobs and Rosenbaum, 1970, 222-72.

———. "Doubl-ling" in *Syntax and Semantics* (Volume I), John Kimball, 1973, 157-86.

———. "Gapping and the Order of Constituents," in Bierwisch and Heidolph, 1970, 249-59.

———. "A Proposed Rule of Tree-Pruning," in Reibel and Schane, 1969, 288-99.

Ruby, Lionel. "Ambiguity," in Anderson and Stageberg, 523-37.

Salomon, Louis B. *Semantics and Common Sense.* New York: Holt, Rinehart and Winston, 1966.

Sampson, Geoffrey. "An Equivocation in an Argument for Generative Semantics," *Foundations of Language,* VII (August, 1971), 426-28.

Sanders, Gerald A. "Invariant Ordering." Bloomington, Ind., Indiana University Linguistics Club, 1970.

———. "Some General Grammatical Processes in English." Bloomington, Ind., Indiana University Linguistics Club, 1968.

Sapir, Edward. *Language.* New York-Harcourt, Brace and Company, 1921.

Schagrin, Morton. *The Language of Logic.* New York: Random House, 1968.

Schank, Roger, Larry Tesler, and Sylvia Weber. *Spinoza II: Conceptual Case-based Natural Language Analysis,* Stanford Artificial Intelligence Project, Memo Aim-109 (1970).

Schmerling, Susan F. "Presupposition and the Notion of Normal Stress," in 1971, Adams *et al.,* 242-53.

Searle, John. "Chomsky's Revolution in Linguistics," in *The New York Review of Books,* June 29, 1972.

Searle, John R. "The Problem of Proper Names," in Steinberg and Jakobovits, 1971, 134-41; a section of *Speech Acts: An Essay in the Philosophy of Language,* by John R. Searle, Cambridge: Cambridge University Press, 1969.

Sebeok, Thomas (ed.). *Current Trends in Linguistics, Volume III, Theoretical Considerations.* The Hague: Mouton, 1966.

Sgall, Petr. "L'Ordre des Mots et la Sémantique," in Kiefer, 1969, 231-40.

Shenker, Israel. "Former Chomsky Disciples Hurl Harsh Words at the Master," in *The New York Times,* September 10, 1972.

Shopen, Tim. "Logical Equivalence is not Semantic Equivalence," in Peranteau, *et al.,* 1972, 340-50.

Shroyer, Thomas G. "An Investigation of the Semantics of English as a Proposed Basis for Language Curriculum Materials." Unpublished Ph.D. dissertation, Ohio State University, 1969.

Smith, Carlota S. "Ambiguous Sentences with *And,*" in Reibel and Schane, 1969, 75-79.

———. "A Class of Complex Modifiers in English," *Language,* XL (January-March, 1964), 37-52.

Stageberg, Norman C. "Ambiguity in College Writing (To a College Freshman)," in Anderson and Stageberg, 473-87.

———. "Some Structural Ambiguities," *The English Journal,* XLVII (November, 1958), 479-86.

———. "Structural Ambiguity for English Teachers," *Teaching the Teacher of English,* Oscar M. Haugh (ed.), Champaign-NCTE, March 1968, 29-34.

———. "Structural Ambiguity in the Noun Phrase," *TESOL Quarterly,* II (December, 1968), 232-39.

———. "Structural Ambiguity: Some Sources," *The English Journal,* LV (May, 1966), 558-63.

Steinberg, D. C., and L. A. Jakobovits (eds.). *Semantics: An Interdisciplinary Reader in Philosophy, Linguistics and Psychology.* Cambridge: Cambridge University Press, 1971.

Steinberg, Danny. "Psychology: Overview," in Steinberg and Jakobovits, 1971, 485-96.

Stine, Philip Clare. "The Instrumental Case in Thai: A Study of Syntax and Semantics in a Generative Model." Unpublished Ph.D. dissertation, University of Michigan, 1968.

Stockwell, Robert P., Paul Schachter, and Barbara Hall Partee. *Integration of Transformational Theories on English Syntax.* Bedford, Mass.: United States Air Force, 1968.

Stratton, Charles R. "The Pathological Case," *Working Papers in Linguistics,* Report No. 10, (Computer and Information Science Research Center of Ohio State University, 1971), 221-30; also read at the 46th Annual Meeting of the Linguistic Society of America, St. Louis, Missouri, December 29, 1971.

Strawson, P. F. "Identifying Reference and Truth-Values," in Steinberg and Jakobovits, 1971, pp. 86-99; reprinted from *Theonia,* XXX (1964), 96-118.

Taylor, Irving A. "Patterns of General Semantics, Perception, and Creativity," *Etc.,* XXIX (June, 1972), 123-32.

Teramura, Hideo. "A List of Case Particles." Unpublished paper, 1970.

Thompson, Sandra Annear. "The Deep Structure of Relative Clauses," in Fillmore and Langendoen, 1971, 78-94.

Thurman, Kelly (ed.). *Semantics.* Boston: Houghton Mifflin, 1960.

Ullman, Stephen. *The Principles of Semantics.* New York: Barnes and Noble, 1957.

———. "Semantic Universals," in Greenberg, 1966, 217-262.

Vendler, Zeno. "Singular Terms," in Steinberg and Jakobovits, 1971, 115-33; reprinted from *Linguistics in Philosophy*, by Zeno Vendler, Ithaca, N.Y.: Cornell University, 1967.

Vermazen, Bruce. "Semantics and Semantics," *Foundations of Language,* VII (November, 1971), 539-55.

Vigo, Anthony W. *"Have* and *be:* Some Observations on Relationships Among Cases." Unpublished paper, 1970.

Wall, Robert. "Selectional Restrictions on Subjects and Objects of Transitive Verbs." Bloomington, Ind., Indiana University Linguistics Club, 1968.

Walmsley, John B. "The English Comitative Case and the Concept of Deep Structure," *Foundations of Language,* VII (November, 1971), 493-507.

Wardhaugh, Ronald. *Introduction to Linguistics.* New York: McGraw-Hill, 1972.

Weigl, E. "A Neuropsychological Contribution to the Problem of Semantics," in Bierwisch and Heidolph, 1970, 340-44.

Weinreich, Uriel. "Lexicographic Definition in Descriptive Semantics," in Householder and Saporta, 1962, 25-44.

———. "On the Semantic Structure of Language," in Greenberg, 1966, 142-216.

———. "Explorations in Semantic Theory," in Sebeok, 1966, pp. 395-477; also in Steinberg and Jakobovits, 1971, 308-28 (this is a shortened version).

Westandorf, Sister Olivia. "The Semantics of Slavery," *Etc.,* XXIX (March, 1972), 27-33.

Wiggins, David. "A Reply to Mr. Alston," in Steinberg and Jakobovits, 1971, 48-52.

———. "On Sentence-Sense, Word-Sense, and Difference of Word Sense: Towards a Philosophical Theory of Dictionaries," in Steinberg and Jakobovits, 1971, 14-34; originally an address given to the Oberlin Philosophy Colloquium in 1968.

Winter, Werner. "Transforms Without Kernels," *Language,* XLI (July-September, 1965), 484-89.

Yamanashi, Masa-Aki. "Lexical Decomposition and Implied Proposition," in Peranteau, *et al.,* 1972, 388-401.

Ziff, Paul. "On H. P. Grice's Account of Meaning," in Steinberg and Jakobovits, 1971, pp. 60-65; reprinted from *Analysis,* XXVIII (October, 1967), 1-8.

———. *Semantic Analysis.* Ithaca, N.Y.: Cornell University Press, 1960.

———. "On Understanding 'Understanding Utterances,'" in Fodor and Katz, 1964, 390-99.

Zwicky, Arnold M. "Linguistics as Chemistry: The Substance Theory of Semantic Primes," *Working Papers in Linguistics*, Report No. 8, (Computer and Information Science Research Center of Ohio State University, 1971), 111-35.

———. "In a Manner of Speaking," *Working Papers in Linguistics*, Report No. 8, (Computer and Information Science Research Center of Ohio State University, 1971), 186-97.

———. "Remarks on Directionality," *Working Papers in Linguistics*, Report No. 8, (Computer and Information Science Research Center of Ohio State University, 1971), 156-63.

———. "On Casual Speech," in Peranteau, *et al.*, 1972, 607-15.

———. "On Reported Speech," in Fillmore and Langendoen, 1971, 72-77.

Zwicky, Arnold M., and Ann D. Zwicky. "How Come and What For," *Working Papers in Linguistics*, Report No. 8, (Computer and Information Science Research Center of Ohio State University, 1971), 173-85.